To Nancy Dobbratz

with all that glitters

ELTON
Captain Fantastic on the Yellow Brick Road
JOHN

GILLIAN G. GAAR

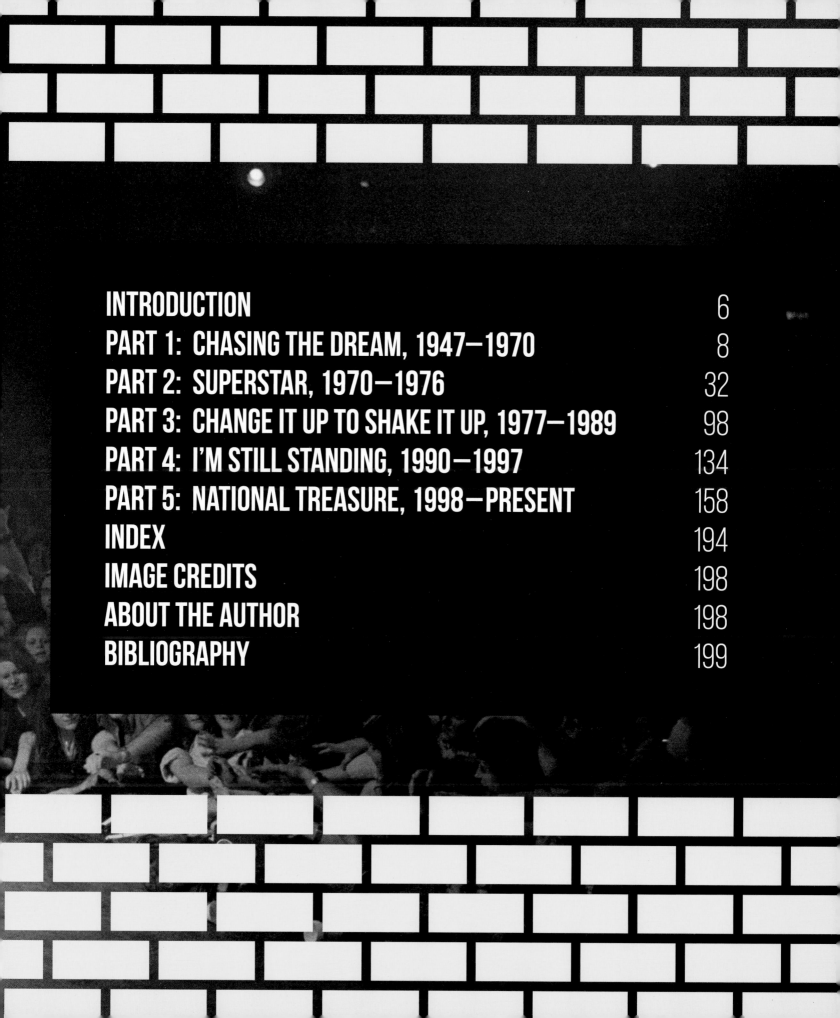

INTRODUCTION

Over the course of a career that's spanned nearly six decades, Elton John has been feted with just about every accolade possible: from gold and platinum record awards, to a shelf filled with Grammys, Tonys, and Oscars, to a knighthood. And he shows no signs of slowing down. When the COVID pandemic put his "Farewell Yellow Brick Road" tour on hold, he used the time to put together a new album (*The Lockdown Sessions*). At the time of this writing, he had a new musical, *The Devil Wears Prada* (music by Elton, lyrics by Shaina Taub), scheduled to open in Chicago in the summer of 2022, en route to Broadway. And though his large-scale touring days may be coming to an end (in favor of spending more time at home with his sons), he surely won't be putting live performance behind him for good.

Even those who aren't overly familiar with his accomplishments will likely recognize a few of his career high points. "Crocodile Rock." His scene-stealing Pinball Wizard in *Tommy. The Lion King*. Performing "Candle in the Wind" at Princess Diana's funeral. But there's always been more to this master showman than meets the eye. Behind the glittering persona he adopts onstage is a man who spent years perfecting his craft before he found international stardom, toiling in clubs with long-forgotten bands, serving as an anonymous session musician on other performers'

hit records, still working under his birth name, Reginald Dwight. And even after finding fame, his work ethic didn't let him slow down. If he wasn't making music himself, there were new acts to produce and promote, a record label to run, a football club to oversee, charity work to undertake. And always, new music to seek out and listen to.

Elton John picks seventy-five key moments in a life full of incident. You'll find significant record releases of course, but not just the hits; Elton released his first vinyl record in 1965. The numerous entries about his years of superstardom in the 1970s are balanced by the years of accomplishment that were still to come, as the man with the Midas touch on the pop charts found similar success in the realm of musicals and soundtracks, his personal life stabilized, and his charity work expanded due to his establishing the Elton John AIDS Foundation.

But it's Elton's own music, and performing, that forms the heart of this story. His 1970s hits comprise the majority of his setlists today, but there's much more to learn about this inveterate music man: his first demos with his longtime lyricist Bernie Taupin, his "lost" psychedelic album *Regimental Sgt. Zippo*, the sessions with "Philly soul" producer Thom Bell where he didn't even play the piano, the stunning performances with the Melbourne

Symphony Orchestra, the remix albums, and the numerous collaborations with performers ranging from Kiki Dee to Leon Russell to Kate Bush to Eddie Vedder. For Elton John, life has always been about the song. And he's always looking for the next one to sing.

PART 1

CHASING THE DREAM, 1947—1970

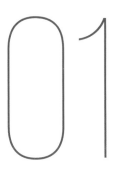

01

. . . .

"IT'S A BOY, MRS. DWIGHT"

. . . .

ELTON ARRIVES ON PLANET EARTH

. . . .

MARCH 25, 1947

Elton John began his life as Reginald Kenneth Dwight, born on March 25, 1947, in Pinner, a suburb of London. He was the only child of Stanley Dwight, a career officer in the Royal Air Force, and Sheila Eileen (née Harris). The two had met in 1942, when Stanley had just joined the RAF, and Sheila had a job delivering milk; they married in 1945.

The family lived with Sheila's mother Ivy and her second husband, Horace, at 55 Pinner Hill Road. Stanley's RAF postings meant he was frequently out of town, to Elton's relief, as his parents argued incessantly when together. To escape the fraught atmosphere, Elton would seek shelter in his room, taking comfort in his toys, comics, and books, creating his own inner world. His parents finally divorced when Elton was thirteen.

But music provided a welcome respite from the domestic turmoil. Both of Elton's parents liked music. Stanley's father Edwin had played soprano cornet, and Stanley had met his future wife at a local dance where he was playing in his own band. As Elton recalled of the household atmosphere, if the radio wasn't playing, there was a record spinning on the radiogram. Frank Sinatra, Rosemary Clooney, Frankie Laine, Jo Stafford, easy-listening shows like *Housewives' Choice* and *Music While You Work*—Elton absorbed it all.

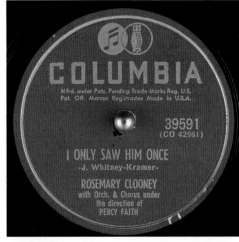

Elton recalled that if the radio wasn't playing in the Dwight home, there was a record spinning on the radiogram.

Elton found an unlikely mentor in Winifred Atwell, a Trinidad-born piano player and hit artist whose specialty was playing two pianos: classical on a grand and ragtime on an upright.

He soon developed a keen interest in records. And not just the music on the discs; he studied the labels, memorizing the names of the artists, songwriters, publishers, and record companies, jotting all the information down and memorizing it. A lifelong obsession with statistics had begun.

And he wasn't just *listening* to music. Ivy owned a piano, and before he entered school, Elton began picking out tunes by ear on the instrument. Elton began taking piano lessons at age seven. Soon he was playing well enough to entertain at weddings and other functions. When his parents had parties, they'd often wake their young son and have him come downstairs to play for their guests.

He found an unlikely inspiration in Winifred Atwell, a Trinidad-born piano player who came to the UK in 1946. A hit artist in the 1950s, her specialty was playing two pianos: classical music on a grand and ragtime on a cheap upright. In a flamboyant gesture that the superstar Elton would appreciate, her hands were insured by Lloyd's of London for £40,000 (she was also forbidden to wash dishes). Elton loved

watching her on television, as she looked like she was having such fun. When he became famous, he met Winifred for tea while visiting Australia, where she had moved.

At age eleven, Elton won a place at the Royal Academy of Music, which he attended—more or less—for five years every Saturday. He enjoyed learning about classical music and singing in the choir, but was more lackadaisical about his homework. Some days he skipped school altogether. Nonetheless, his education in the classics would give his own music a distinctive touch.

Music and parental arguments aside, Elton's childhood was fairly ordinary. Though shy and self-conscious about his weight, he had friends at school and developed a keen interest in sports and their relevant statistics.

And then came a musical eruption that turned his world upside down.

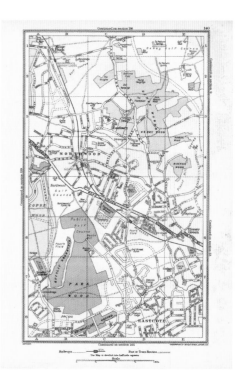

Elton John began his life in Pinner, a suburb of London.

02

. . . .

HAIL, HAIL, ROCK 'N' ROLL!

. . . .

A LIFE-CHANGING ENCOUNTER WITH THE KING

. . . .

SPRING 1956

By his early teens, Elton was keenly interested in music and a more than proficient piano player. But the arrival of Elvis Presley and the rise of rock 'n' roll changed everything. Elton had never imagined that music could be so enthralling. He became determined to be a part of this magic world.

It's hard for a twenty-first-century audience to fully appreciate the seismic impact that Elvis Presley had when he first exploded onto the music scene. He wasn't just considered a new and different kind of performer—he was shocking and outrageous, even potentially dangerous. Elton had been taken by Elvis even before hearing a note of his music, spellbound by a photo of the young Presley that he'd seen in *Life* magazine while waiting to get his hair cut at the barber. Elvis's flashy dress and hairstyle made him seem like he'd been beamed here from outer space. Who was this fabulous creature?

Later, Elton was thrilled to find that his mother had brought home a copy of Elvis's latest single, "Heartbreak Hotel." Its heavy, echo-laden sound was like nothing else heard on the radio, and Elvis's slurring, Southern accent made it hard to understand what he was singing, making the song even more mysterious.

Elvis was just the start. "Rock and roll was like a bomb that wouldn't stop going off," Elton wrote in his memoir *Me*. Elvis was quickly followed by the likes of Chuck Berry, Eddie Cochran, Gene Vincent, and Carl Perkins, many of whom Elton was later able to see at his local theater. And there was more to rock 'n' roll than just the music. The clothes, the culture, and the defiant attitude of the genre were irresistible to a generation coming of age in drab, postwar Britain. That the music originated in America, mythical land of plenty, made it seem even more exotic.

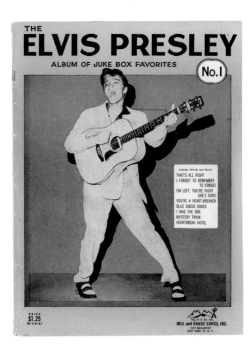

The arrival of Elvis and rock 'n' roll changed everything for Elton. He had never imagined music could be so enthralling.

Elton was especially fascinated by Jerry Lee Lewis and Little Richard, both of whom played piano, pounding the instrument with the same power and aggression as any electric guitar player. It was a far cry from Winifred Atwell. Though he needed eyeglasses only for reading, Elton began wearing them all the time, thinking they made him look like Buddy Holly. Unfortunately, wearing prescription lenses all the time damaged his eyesight, and eventually he would need to wear glasses not only as a fashion accessory, but to see properly.

Elton was especially fascinated by Jerry Lee Lewis and Little Richard, both of whom played piano with the same aggression as any guitar player.

Unlike other parents who shunned the music, Elton's mother and stepfather, Fred Farebrother (whom Elton playfully called "Derf," Fred spelled backward), liked rock 'n' roll, and encouraged his interest in performing. Derf got Elton his first professional gig at a local pub, the Northwood Hills Hotel, playing piano for a pound a night, plus tips. It was an invaluable experience, teaching him how to perform for a lively, occasionally raucous audience, playing a diverse repertoire that encompassed standards, a little rock 'n' roll, and traditional pub singalongs like "Down at the Old Bull and Bush."

He also formed a band with fellow students called the Corvettes. The short-lived group played local youth clubs and generally received soft drinks as payment. In a hint of the later showmanship to come, Elton adopted the habit of kicking away his piano bench during the show, in the fashion of Jerry Lee Lewis. The more he performed, the more Elton realized that this was the path he wanted to follow. In March 1965, with the approval of his mother and stepfather (and to the dismay of his father, who thought his son should take up a more conventional profession), he decided to leave Pinner County Grammar School and pursue a career in the music business. Elton was on his way.

Though he needed eyeglasses only for reading, Elton began wearing them all the time, thinking they made him look like Buddy Holly.

03

ELTON'S VINYL DEBUT

"COME BACK BABY"

JULY 23, 1965 (UK RELEASE)

Publicity photo of Bluesology.

Just four months after Elton left school he released his very first single with his new band, Bluesology. It may not have been a very auspicious start, but it was an important first step.

Elton's cousin, Roy Dwight, a former footballer for Fulham FC, had contacts in the music business and helped Elton get a job at the publishing company Mills Music. He worked as an office boy, making tea, filling orders for sheet music, and mailing packages. It wasn't prestigious, but the office was located on Denmark Street, then a hub of London's music industry, and Elton loved the atmosphere.

By then, he'd started a new band with Stuart Brown, a fellow member of the Corvettes. Bluesology's name was inspired by guitarist Django Reinhardt's album *Djangology* and was meant to be a serious blues group, playing covers of Jimmy Witherspoon and J. B. Lenoir. Their drummer, Mick Inkpen, worked for a jeweler, Arnold Tendler, who became the band's manager. He put up the money for a demo, which attracted the attention of Fontana Records.

"Come Back Baby" was written by Elton, who also sang lead; Brown, the usual lead singer, couldn't reach the high notes. It's a pleasant song, if closer to

Bluesology was meant to be a serious blues group, covering the likes of Jimmy Witherspoon and J. B. Lenoir.

Reissue of the first Bluesology single.

Bluesology became the backing group for six-foot-seven blues singer Long John Baldry.

the girl-group pop of the Shirelles than a bona fide blues number. But there was a bit of a blues swing in the group's second single, "Mr. Frantic," again written and sung by Elton, and released by Fontana in February 1966.

Neither single made an impression and Fontana dropped the group. But they kept busy as a live act, enabling Elton to quit his job at Mills Music. The band opened for the Animals, Stevie Wonder, and Little Richard, and backed touring acts like Patti LaBelle and the Bluebells, Fontella Bass, and Billy Stewart. Elton was thrilled to tour with acts whose records he'd studied so assiduously.

Bluesology went on to tour Europe. Elton later joked that he was probably the only British musician to play Hamburg's notorious red-light district and not lose his virginity. But he had doubts about how far the group could go. "Most of the guys were happy with their thirty quid a week and didn't have any real ambition," he later said. His only contribution to the group's third single, "Since I Found You Baby," released in October 1967, was playing keyboards.

By then, Bluesology had become the backing group for a six-foot-seven blues singer and musician named Long John Baldry. Elton enjoyed working with a musician he considered a blues legend and who'd previously performed in Alexis Korner's Blues Incorporated. But that changed when Baldry had an unexpected British #1 in 1967 with the single "Let the Heartaches Begin," a song invariably described with the word

schmaltzy ("Hey Lord, You Made the Night Too Long," the B-side of non-UK pressings, was co-written by Baldry, Tony Macaulay, and Elton, credited as Reg Dwight). Due to its string arrangement, Baldry sang to a backing tape when performing the song live, while the rest of the band stayed on stage, trying to look inconspicuous. Elton's unhappiness with the situation made him realize it was time to move on.

In December 1967, he told the other band members he was leaving, taking two of the members' names—Elton Dean and John Baldry—for his own new identity. While he had no definite plans, he did have a new songwriting partner, and their work together seemed to have real potential.

04

"I'M A MUSICAL MOUTHPIECE FOR HIS LYRICS"

THE AD THAT CREATED THE ELTON JOHN / BERNIE TAUPIN SONGWRITING TEAM

JUNE 17, 1967

In June 1967, Elton was on the road with Bluesology in Newcastle when he saw an ad in the music weekly *New Musical Express* that would change his life.

"LIBERTY WANTS TALENT" read the bold type in *NME*'s June 17, 1967, issue, announcing that Liberty Records was on the lookout for singers, musicians, and composers. Elton had been unhappy that Long John Baldry had taken over most singing duties with Bluesology, leaving him with little to do, and he felt he needed to make a move. He'd unsuccessfully applied for a job at Phillips Records. Maybe he'd have better luck with Liberty.

It didn't seem so at first. Elton sent off a letter, and was called in to meet with Liberty's A&R rep, Ray Williams, at his office in London's tony Mayfair district. Elton sat at the piano and played the Jim Reeves weepy "He'll Have to Go"— not exactly the new sound Williams was looking for. But he was intrigued by Elton: by the breadth of his musical knowledge and particularly his skill as a pianist. He decided to have Elton record a few demos. But neither Liberty Records, nor their publishing company, Metric Music, wanted to sign him.

Elton was discouraged when Williams gave him the bad news. Almost as an afterthought, Williams handed him an envelope. Elton had mentioned that he could write music, but had little confidence in his skills as a lyricist. Williams had received a packet of lyrics from another young man who'd answered the Liberty ad, saying he could write lyrics but not music. Why didn't Elton take a look at what had been sent in and see what he thought?

The lyrics were by Bernie Taupin, then working on a chicken farm in Owmby-by-Spital. Bernard John Taupin was born on May 22, 1950, at Flatters Farmhouse, located between the towns of Anwick and Sleaford in Lincolnshire. An avid reader, he had a special

The *New Musical Express* ad that changed Elton's life.

Elton's take on Jim Reeves' weepy "He'll Have to Go" intrigued Liberty A&R rep Ray Williams.

fascination for the stories and legends of the American West. He was equally interested in music, and had been particularly inspired by Bob Dylan, whose imaginative wordplay showed Bernie that lyrics could be more than moon-and-June cliches; they could also be artistic.

But he found little outlet for his nascent ambitions. A brief stint at a newspaper printing shop hadn't led to a hoped-for writing gig, and now he was stuck at the chicken farm. Figuring he had nothing to lose, he prepared an envelope to send to Liberty, placing it on the mantelpiece but forgetting about it. Luckily, his mother noticed it sitting there and mailed it off for him.

Elton looked through the lyrics with fanciful names like "Swan Queen of the Laughing Lake" and "The Year of the Teddy Bear." He sat down at the piano and immediately came up with a melody for a lyric called "Scarecrow." It was a foretaste of how the two would work together, Bernie writing the lyrics and then handing them off to Elton.

After six weeks, the two finally met in person when Bernie came to London. They went for coffee at the Lancaster Grill on Tottenham Court Road to discuss their potential future. They hit it off and a partnership was born. As Elton later described the meeting to DJ Andy Peebles, "He came down with this tatty little suitcase from Lincoln and we decided to try and make a go of it."

Elton with lyricist Bernie Taupin shortly after they signed contracts with Dick James Music in 1968.

05

....

SESSION MAN

....

"DELILAH"
(BY TOM JONES)

As he worked to build his own career, Elton took jobs as a session player, appearing on hit singles like "Delilah" by Welsh heartthrob Tom Jones (pictured).

....

FEBRUARY 1968
(UK RELEASE)

Years before Elton John began racking up hits of his own, future fans were unwittingly listening to him as a backing vocalist and musician on other artists' records.

As he worked to build his own career as a songwriter and performer, Elton took on extra work as a session player to help pay the bills. His list of credits is impressive: From 1968 to 1970 he ended up appearing on hit singles like Tom Jones's "Delilah" and "Daughter of Darkness" (on backing vocals); the Hollies' "He Ain't Heavy, He's My Brother"

(on piano); the Scaffold's "Lily the Pink" and "Gin Gan Goolie" (backing vocals); and the Barron Knights' "An Olympic Record" (piano). His first appearances on *Top of the Pops* were in a similar capacity, providing backing vocals for the Brotherhood of Man and Pickettywitch when they were featured on the long-running television program.

Elton enjoyed the work, not only for the extra money (£3 an hour for a three-hour session), but also because it made him an incredibly versatile musician, as he was called upon to sing and play a

variety of styles. He had even more fun recording cover songs for budget compilations like *Chartbusters* and *Hit Parade* that featured re-recordings of current hits.

Elton was up for tackling anything. His lead vocals can be easily recognized on his covers of "Bridge Over Trouble Water" (Simon and Garfunkel), "Lady D'Arbanville" (Cat Stevens), "Signed, Sealed, Delivered" (Stevie Wonder), and "Spirit in the Sky" (Norman Greenbaum). For a longtime Beatles fan, a cover of Badfinger's "Come and Get It" (written by Paul McCartney) was a logical choice. Less so was the decision to have a British white man sing Nina Simone's "To Be Young, Gifted and Black." But he turns in a creditable version, nonetheless, giving the song a touch of reggae.

Even after he'd released his own albums and appeared on *Top of the Pops* in his own right, he couldn't resist the occasional bit of session work. Right before he left for his first American tour in the fall of 1970, he recorded covers of "In the Summertime" (Mungo Jerry) and "Let's Work Together" (Canned Heat). "It was, as usual, a hoot," he said in his memoir.

After Elton became famous, such tracks were compiled on releases like *Reg Dwight's Piano Goes Pop* and *Legendary Covers '69/'70*. The songs can also be found on YouTube.

Elton circa 1969 in London.

06

• • • • • • • • • • • • • • •

THE LOST ALBUM

• • • • • • • • • • • • • • •

REGIMENTAL SGT. ZIPPO

• • • • • • • • • • • • • • •

NOVEMBER 1967–MAY 1968
(RECORDING)

Elton John's real first album, *Regimental Sgt. Zippo*, established him as one of England's most promising rising talents. The melodicism and the lyrical inventiveness also made the songwriting team of John/Taupin one to watch. Clearly, these two young men were destined for great things.

Well, that's how it might have played out in a parallel universe. In the real universe, *Empty Sky* (1969) was of course Elton's debut album. But *Regimental Sgt. Zippo*, recorded from November 1967 to May 1968, could well have been the debut.

Unlike the work-for-hire songs they wrote to try to entice middle-of-the-road entertainers to record them, the *Sgt. Zippo* songs reflected Elton's and Bernie's own aesthetic. They were more sophisticated and lyrically fanciful, as evidenced by song titles like "And the Clock Goes Around" and "Tartan Coloured Lady."

"When I Was Tealby Abbey" is catchy psychedelic pop, with the surreal twist of being sung from the perspective of the titular abbey itself. "Sitting Doing Nothing" features splendid harmonies, with the lyrics written by Elton for a change, and the music by Caleb Quaye; the two also wrote "You'll Be Sorry to See Me Go," one of the harder-rocking tracks. The trippy title track not only

"The lost album" got a limited vinyl release for Record Store Day 2021—"In beautiful swinging mono."

references the Beatles' *Sgt. Pepper's Lonely Hearts Club Band* and the very English whimsy of their single "Penny Lane," but also Elton's father's own military career. Along with Elton (on a variety of keyboards) and Quaye (guitar, flute, percussion, and backing vocals), other musicians included future Elton John Band bassist Dee Murray, and drummer Dave Hynes.

It's not clear how close *Sgt. Zippo* came to being released at the time. All of its tracks, aside from "You'll Be Sorry to See Me Go," appeared on 2020's *Jewel Box* set, though some only in demo form. Final versions of all songs were eventually issued the following year on a vinyl release for Record Store Day in a limited run of seven thousand copies– "In beautiful swinging mono," as a label on the shrinkwrap put it. The swirly, colorful cover art was based on a black-and-white illustration artist David Larkham had designed back in 1969 for the press kit accompanying the *Empty Sky* release. The illustration was based on a photo Larkham had taken in 1968 ("That was how he looked in 1968, with the horseshoe moustache"), and added the faces of Bernie and Dick James Music promotions man Steve Brown to the phantasmagorical mix.

January 1968 in the Heath section of London.

ELTON GOES SOLO

"I'VE BEEN LOVING YOU"

MARCH 1, 1968
(UK RELEASE)

"HEAR THE GREATEST PERFORMANCE ON A 'FIRST' DISC," was the bold assertion in the ad that ran in the March 2, 1968 edition of *New Musical Express*. "You have been warned! ELTON JOHN is 1968's great new talent." Three years after his first single release as a member of Bluesology, Elton had finally released a single under his own name.

Though Liberty Records had turned him down, Ray Williams co-owned a publishing company, Niraki Music, with songwriters Nicky James and Kirk Duncan, and he suggested Elton collaborate with them. Niraki was overseen by another publishing company, Gralto, which was itself managed by Dick James Music (DJM). Dick James was one of the most successful publishers in the industry, co-owning the Beatles' publishing company, Northern Songs.

DJM's offices had a small studio that Elton and Bernie used to record demos, working with engineer Caleb Quaye, who'd been part of the revolving cast of Bluesology members. When they were caught recording without authorization, Quaye, hoping to save his job, played their demos to James and his son Stephen. The ploy worked, and Elton and Bernie were signed to a publishing deal, getting a joint advance and a weekly wage: £10 for Bernie, and £15 for Elton, who played on sessions for other DJM artists. Now that Elton was fully free of Bluesology, Bernie quit the chicken farm, and they moved into Elton's family home in suburban Northwood Hills.

The two worked at writing songs for other artists. Actor Edward Woodward would pick their "The Tide Will Turn for Rebecca" for his 1970 album *This Man Alone*. They scored no hits, but the demos did attract interest in Elton's voice. Tony Hatch, who wrote the Petula Clark hit "Downtown," advised Stephen

James that the songwriting team's songs were "too original" for other artists, and might be more successful if recorded by Elton himself. So DJM signed him as a recording artist. Elton, thinking of himself primarily as a songwriter, felt that recording his own work might help draw more attention to his songs.

"I've Been Loving You," released on Philips Records, was written solely by Elton, though Bernie was credited as co-songwriter so he could share in any royalties. It's a pleasant, middle-of-the-road number, Elton imbuing his vocal with perhaps more drama than the lyric requires. Much the same could be said of the B-side, "Here's to the Next Time" (also written solely by Elton), though it has a stronger vocal and good harmonies. The song failed to attract any interest, though in 1976, the Canadian band Wednesday would have a Top 10 hit with it, renaming it "Loving You Baby."

The problem was that the songs had no personality. At the time, Elton and Bernie were excited by the creativity of artists like The Beatles, Cat Stevens, the Moody Blues, and Leonard Cohen, but none of those influences found their way into their own work—yet. "I've Been Loving You" was more akin to the mainstream songs they hoped another artist would record, as opposed to a song that truly expressed their own feelings. Indeed, Bernie later said that was why he was glad the single had failed: "If it had been successful it might have put us on a completely different trajectory. It wasn't what we aspired to and was simply an appeasement to those who saw us more as Engelbert Humperdinck than Pink Floyd." Their creative breakthrough was still to come.

PHILIPS

BF 1643
326 855 BF

Dick James
Music

45

MONO
▽

A

© 1968

326 855 1F

I'VE BEEN LOVING YOU
(Elton John/Bernie Taupin)
ELTON JOHN
A 'THIS' Production

HEAR THE GREATEST PERFORMANCE ON A 'FIRST' DISC

ELTON JOHN

'I'VE BEEN LOVING YOU'

A
"THIS"
PRODUCTION

Produced by
CALEB

Released on
PHILIPS
BF 1643

Published by
DICK JAMES MUSIC

You have been warned ! ELTON JOHN is 1968's great new talent

Early publicity photo, taken on
Hampstead Heath.

"I've Been Loving You," released on Philips Records,
was written solely by Elton, though Bernie was
credited as co-songwriter.

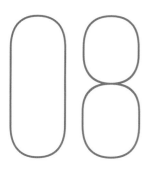

08

ELTON'S FIRST LONG-PLAYER

EMPTY SKY

JUNE 6, 1969 (UK RELEASE)

JANUARY 13, 1975 (US RELEASE)

Elton's initial singles hadn't made much of a splash. But DJM had faith in his talent. Steve Brown, who handled promotions for DJM, was supportive of the new direction they'd taken in songs like "Lady Samantha" (Elton's second single) and urged Dick James to release a full album by Elton on the newly created DJM Records label.

With Brown producing, *Empty Sky* was recorded at DJM's own studio; if the sessions ran late, meaning Elton and Bernie missed the last train home, Brown put them up for the night at his father's home. Relishing the opportunity to make a full album, the musical backing was made more elaborate. "We collectively threw everything we could at the new songs," Elton said. After all, he thought, who knew if he'd get to make another album? Better pull out all the stops while he could.

"Skyline Pigeon," *Empty Sky*'s strongest production, became the album's best-known track. Elton's was the second released version of the song, which had previously come out as a single by Roger James Cook (Elton never released the song as a single himself). Elton's version is the only track on the album where he's the sole performer, playing harpsichord and organ, while singing a plaintive lyric, first from the point of view of the titular pigeon begging for release ("Let me fly to distant lands"), then a third-person perspective of the bird in flight. The "bird" also works as a metaphor for anyone feeling trapped by their circumstances, a theme that crops up in other songs on the album.

The UK and US album sleeves.

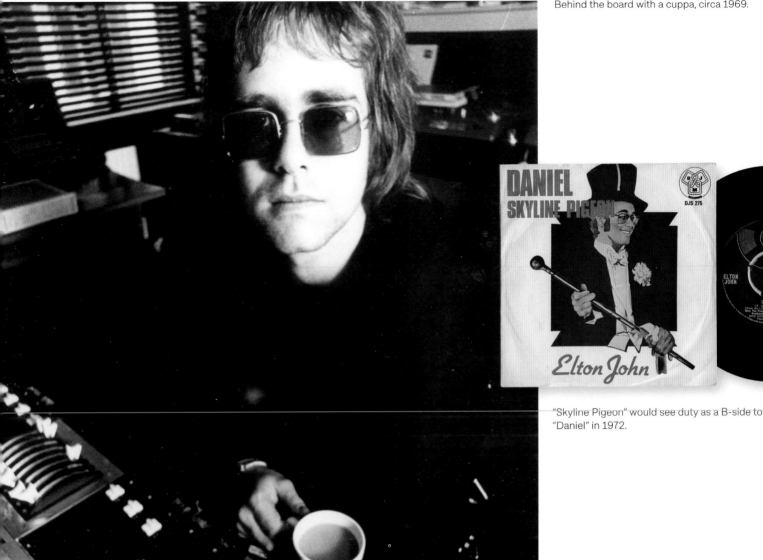

Behind the board with a cuppa, circa 1969.

"Skyline Pigeon" would see duty as a B-side to "Daniel" in 1972.

As Elton and Bernie viewed *Empty Sky* as more of a showcase for their own work than an album meant to promote Elton as a performer, the songs embraced a variety of styles. The folk of the ecologically minded "Lady What's Tomorrow" contrasted with the harder rock of the title track, clearly an homage to the Rolling Stones. Bernie's interest in myths and legends is on full display in the contemplative "Val-Hala" (referring to Valhalla, the heavenly home for warriors in Norse mythology), "The Scaffold" (a balladeering number with references to Eldorado and the fearsome Minotaur), and "Western Ford Gateway" (a forlorn depiction of tavern brawls and shootouts). The closing track, "Gulliver"/"Hay Chewed"/"Reprise," cleverly starts as a eulogy to Bernie's father's dog, then ends with a musical recap of the album's other tracks.

Empty Sky was initially released only in the UK, and DJM ponied up the money to pay for large ads posted on the back of London's red double-decker buses. But it made no impression on the charts and received mixed reviews; London's *Evening Standard* called it "nicely recorded but unadventurous." Nonetheless, Elton saw it as a step forward, and with an album to promote, he returned to live performing.

The album wasn't released in the US until 1975, featuring a different cover than the UK release. By then, Elton's popularity sent it all the way to #6.

09

"IS THIS THE YEAR OF ELTON JOHN?"

ELTON JOHN

APRIL 10, 1970 (UK RELEASE)

JULY 22, 1970 (US RELEASE)

Elton John was Elton's make-or-break album. For all the support DJM had given him and Bernie over the years, the company hadn't seen much return on their investment. After the poor performance of *Empty Sky*, Elton had considered moving to another label; Island Records had expressed some interest. But DJM was unwilling to let Elton go and decided to give him another chance.

After hearing the new songs the two were coming up with (in particular, the sterling "Your Song"), Steve Brown decided to step aside as producer and bring in someone more experienced. He'd already chosen Paul Buckmaster, who'd done the arrangements for David Bowie's first hit, "Space Oddity," to serve in the same capacity for Elton's next album. Buckmaster recommended that the single's producer, Gus Dudgeon, to take on the job. Dudgeon agreed—and became Elton's producer for the next six years.

DJM also put up the money for the album to be recorded in a proper studio, Trident, in London's Soho neighborhood. It was recorded quickly, over the course of a week in January 1970; for Elton, the most nerve-wracking part came when he had to play the piano, live, with the orchestra ("I was petrified"). But the sessions were carefully planned down to the last detail, and everything ended up coming together in what Elton described as a "weirdly magical" way.

"Border Song" was the first single, previewing the album that would arrive a few weeks later. It's a song heavy with gospel overtones, both musically (the backing choir) and lyrically (with a final verse about racial harmony written by Elton). And if it didn't set the charts alight, it did lead to Elton's first solo appearance on *Top of the Pops*.

The cover of *Elton John* casts him as a serious young man; the side portrait, in shadow, is the very image of a sensitive

Elton John was recorded quickly. For Elton, the most nerve-wracking part was playing live with an orchestra.

Japanese picture sleeve for "Border Song."

singer-songwriter. Certainly, songs like "I Need You to Turn To" (with Elton playing harpsichord), the somber "Sixty Years On," and "Your Song" fit neatly into that genre. But versatility was always the key to Elton's musicianship, and the more reflective numbers were balanced by the likes of "No Shoe Strings on Louise," a bawdy blues; the rollicking "Take Me to the Pilot," which quickly became an audience favorite (though Bernie always said the lyrics meant nothing, Elton liked the way they flowed); and the closing number, "The King Must Die," a mighty ballad of kingdoms, jugglers, and courtiers. There were weak moments—the heavily romantic "First Episode at Hienton" tends to be mawkish—but it was a confident step forward that benefited from both the superior songs and more professional production and arrangements.

The reviews were good, and the sales gave Elton his first Top 5 hit, with the album peaking at #4 in the US and #5 in the UK. At long last, Elton had the commercial breakthrough he'd been waiting for.

10

"WRITTEN IN FIVE MINUTES, RECORDED IN TWO"

"YOUR SONG"

OCTOBER 26, 1970
(US RELEASE)

JANUARY 7, 1971
(UK RELEASE)

"Your Song" was a turning point in the career of a
young songwriting team. Elton said, "We never
looked back."

By 1970, Elton and Bernie had written dozens of songs together. But they knew "Your Song" was something special even before they recorded it.

The song was written when the two were living with Elton's mother and stepfather in the suburbs. Bernie wrote the lyric at the breakfast table, then passed it to Elton. As Elton looked at Bernie's words, he knew he had to up his game, thinking, "Oh my God, this is such a great lyric, I can't fuck this one up." But the music flowed freely: "It came out in about 20 minutes, and when I was done, I called [Bernie] in, and we both knew."

It's a tender, affecting love song with an air of innocence, as Bernie recognized, telling author Tom Doyle, "It's the voice of someone who hasn't experienced love in any way. It's a very virginal song." It's the song of a would-be lover shyly confessing his feelings, nicely captured in the hesitancy of the line "But then again, no." It's sweet without being cloying, and Paul Buckmaster's string arrangement is simple and tasteful.

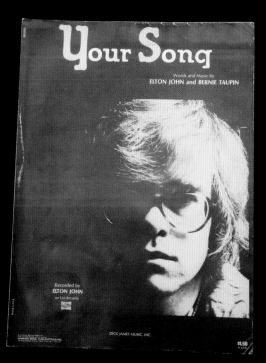

The Hollies told Dick James they'd be interested in covering the song but were told they couldn't. Yet Elton wasn't the first artist to release the song; Three Dog Night featured it on their album *It Ain't Easy*, released in March 1970. When Elton's version was released on a single, first in the US, it wasn't even the A-side; that honor went to "Take Me to the Pilot."

But US DJs began flipping the single over, and it soon began rising on the charts, peaking at #8—Elton's first-ever Top 10 single. When the single was released a few months later in the UK, it also reached the Top 10, peaking at #7. The single's success built nicely on the foundation the *Elton John* album had established.

Other artists have subsequently landed hits on the UK charts with their covers of "Your Song": Billy Paul in 1977, Rod Stewart in 1992, and Ellie Goulding in 2010. In 2012, Elton recorded a new version with opera singer Alessandro Safina as a charity single, which

reached #4 in the UK and had worldwide sales of over three million digital downloads. Lady Gaga's 2018 cover was a Top 40 hit in seven countries, including reaching #21 on *Billboard*'s Pop Digital Songs chart. It's been featured in numerous films and TV shows over the years. One especially memorable appearance of the song was in Baz Luhrmann's 2001 jukebox musical extravaganza *Moulin Rouge!*, where Ewan McGregor, playing a penniless writer, sings the song to woo the affections of Nicole Kidman's courtesan Satine.

"Your Song" was a turning point in the career of the young songwriting team, Elton calling it "a huge step forward in our songwriting. We never looked back from that song."

11

"LADIES AND GENTLEMEN, WE HAVE A NEW MESSIAH IN TOWN!"

THE TROUBADOUR RESIDENCY

....

AUGUST 25–30, 1970

Elton hadn't expected much in the way of success on his first trip to the US, admitting, "The only reason I agreed was that I thought that at least I'd be able to buy some records." Instead, the eight shows he performed at LA's Troubadour club proved to be, as Bernie remembered, "the blue-touch paper for our career."

Things could have turned out very differently. In July 1970, Jeff Beck offered Elton the opportunity to back him on an upcoming US tour. Elton thought it would be a great way to raise his profile in the States. He was mortified when Dick James turned down the offer, and further astonished by James's pronouncement that in six months' time he'd be earning twice as much as Jeff Beck was.

Other factors also came into play. Elton's records had been picked up by Uni Records in the US. The label's president, Russ Regan, was so impressed with Elton's self-titled second album that he quickly set up a showcase at the Troubadour, a legendary LA club that had hosted acts like Joni Mitchell, the Byrds, and Buffalo Springfield (and was also where comedian Lenny Bruce had been arrested for obscenity).

Regan didn't stint on promotion. Elton might have been embarrassed to be met at the airport by a red London double-decker bus with a banner reading "Elton John Has Arrived!" on the side. But his records were in the shops and on the radio, and a star-studded opening night was guaranteed. Elton was plagued by nerves and at one point became so agitated he called Dick James and insisted he was going back to England. James managed to calm him down.

Elton couldn't believe he was headlining over singer-songwriter David Ackles, whom he and Bernie much admired.

On opening night, luminaries like Odetta, Quincy Jones, Randy Newman, and members of the Beach Boys and Three Dog Night could be spotted in the audience. Neil Diamond, another Uni Records artist, graciously agreed to introduce Elton and his band (Dee Murray, bass, and Nigel Olsson, drums).

He started out like you'd expect a singer-songwriter would, with "Your Song." But his attire—yellow overalls, black long-sleeved shirt covered with stars, and white boots featuring green wings—hinted at an inner outrageousness, and he became increasingly wild and aggressive as the set progressed. "When he got to 'Take Me to the Pilot,' the place levitated," Linda Ronstadt later recalled. And when he came to "Burn Down the Mission," he went all out, kicking his piano stool away to the crowd's delight.

A glowing review by Robert Hilburn, rock critic at the *Los Angeles Times*, was the cherry on top: "Rejoice! Rock music, which has been going through a rather uneventful period lately, has a new star." Word of mouth quickly spread, and the rest of the run was a sellout. Elton had lived the showbiz cliché of going on stage a nobody and coming back a star. "I knew this was my big moment and I really went for it," he later reflected. "It was pure rock 'n' roll serendipity. Even before the reviews came in, we knew that something special had happened."

Backstage—and onstage—at the pivotal Troubadour residency.

PART 2

SUPERSTAR, 1970—1976

12

"MUCH SIMPLER AND FUNKIER"

TUMBLEWEED CONNECTION

OCTOBER 30, 1970
(UK RELEASE)

JANUARY 4, 1971
(US RELEASE)

"Your Song" on *Top of the Pops*, January 1971.

Tumbleweed's sleeve reflected the LP's romanticized vision of the American West.

For an album steeped in Americana, it's interesting that *Tumbleweed Connection* was written and recorded before either Elton or Bernie had set foot in the US.

In contrast to the orchestrations found on his previous album, *Tumbleweed* was decidedly stripped down, featuring musicians from Caleb Quaye's latest band, Hookfoot, as well as his touring musicians, Dee Murray and Nigel Olsson. The most obvious influence was the music of The Band, Bob Dylan's backup group who had struck out on their own and found immediate success with their first album, *Music from Big Pink* (1968). Elton and Bernie adored their work and were stunned when the group came into their dressing room following a show at the Electric Factory in Philadelphia in November 1970, asking to hear their latest album (which had not yet been released in the US).

Tumbleweed Connection wasn't deliberately put together as a "concept album," but there is a thematic commonality that links the songs. It's a series of vignettes, a romanticized vision of the American Wild West, replete with outlaws, weary soldiers, and homesteaders. The groundwork for that musical direction had been laid during the *Elton John* sessions, when the basic tracks for "Burn Down the Mission," "Country Comfort," and "Come Down in Time" were recorded. "Country Comfort" is an ode to rural life, where residents forsake modern machinery in favor of an old-fashioned horse. The folky "Come Down in Time" mourns a lost love. "Burn Down the Mission" is the album's standout track, a tour de force about an uprising among the underprivileged, fighting to survive in the land of plenty. It became a live favorite due to its musical intensity.

And then come the gunslingers. Gritty, gospel-flavored rock provides the musical backdrop for both "Ballad of a Well-Known Gun," whose lawless protagonist ends up serving time on the chain gang, and the men who end up dead as the result of a shootout in "Son of Your Father." Moderate-tempo rock underscores "My Father's Gun," about a Confederate soldier eagerly taking up arms to avenge his father's death. Yet there's no glory to be found in war. "Where to Now, St. Peter?" has a dreamy, almost languorous feeling until you take a closer look at the lyrics, sung from the point of view of a wounded soldier, passing from this life to the next. And "Talking Old Soldiers" is a devastating depiction of post-traumatic stress, with a one-time warrior trying to drink away the memories of the friends he lost to the bullet, set to a funereal piano accompaniment.

Not everything ends in tragedy. "Amoreena" is another song about being separated from one's love, but the musical mood is on the upbeat side. And "Love Song" is simply sweet and tender (featuring backing vocals from the song's composer, Lesley Duncan).

No singles were released from the album in the US or UK (though "Country Comfort" was released as a single in Brazil, Australia, and New Zealand). The album itself was another Top 10 hit: #5 in the US, #2 in the UK. It also became Elton's first platinum record, firmly establishing that he was no one-hit wonder. Elton John had arrived, and he was here to stay.

Elton and Bernie cited The Band's landmark *Music from Big Pink* as inspirational.

13

LIVE, FROM COAST TO COAST

THE FIRST LIVE ALBUM:
11-17-70 (US),
17-11-70 (UK)

APRIL 1, 1971 (UK RELEASE)

APRIL 9, 1971 (US RELEASE)

Elton's breakthrough in the States was due to his charisma as a live performer. He had played smaller venues during his first visits to the US, meaning not everybody could see him. Why not make him as accessible as possible, bringing the show into every home in America via a live radio broadcast?

Following Elton's performance at the Santa Monica Civic Auditorium on November 15, 1970, he flew to New York City, and on November 17 walked into A&R Recording Studios at 799 7th Avenue to perform before a specially invited studio audience of around 125 people. It was his first-ever live performance in the Big Apple; his first club dates would follow on November 20 and 21 at the Fillmore East. Elton

was thrilled to learn that the Steinway piano he'd be playing had previously been used by Burt Bacharach.

The thirteen-song set offered a solid, well-rounded look at Elton John, circa 1970. There were three recent singles, including, not surprisingly, his first Top 10 hit, "Your Song"; songs from *Elton John* and the just-released *Tumbleweed Connection*; and a new song, "Indian Sunset." The highlight was a pulse-pounding version of "Burn Down the Mission" that segued into Elvis Presley's "My Baby Left Me" and The Beatles' "Get Back" during the course of its eighteen minutes. And speaking of covers, there's also a riveting version of the Rolling Stones' "Honky Tonk Women," which opens with a great bit of a cappella harmonizing.

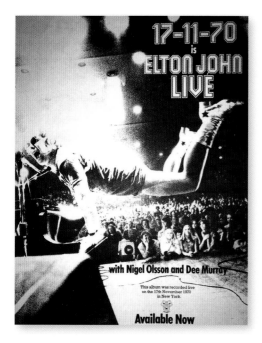

The performance was broadcast live on WABC-FM. There were no plans to release an album. But airing the show on radio allowed eager listeners to record it themselves. Soon bootlegs were appearing in abundance and it was decided that an official album should tap into the market. Given the different style of calendar dating, the album was released as *11-17-70* in the US (where it reached #11) and *17-11-70* in the UK (#20). The striking cover shot was not a photo from the studio performance, but from Elton's Troubadour residency.

However, the studio album featured just six songs from the performance, meaning bootleggers could still take advantage by releasing their own complete versions of the show. A 1996 CD on Rocket Records added one track to the lineup, and in 2017 a new collection, *17-11-70+*, was released on Record Store Day, officially issuing every song from the performance for the first time. (None of the official releases have the show's original running order, an omission curiously not corrected on the 2017 release.)

In any edition, the performance is a fascinating document of the nascent Elton John Band when it solely comprised Elton, bassist Dee Murray, and drummer Nigel Olsson. This was the threesome that conquered America and paved the way for what was to come.

November 1970, a few days before the first live album was cut at New York's A&R Recording Studios before a small audience.

"LIKE A DIARY OF THE LAST YEAR"

MADMAN ACROSS THE WATER

NOVEMBER 5, 1971
(UK RELEASE)

NOVEMBER 15, 1971
(US RELEASE)

If *Tumbleweed Connection* was a portrait of America's mythic past, *Madman Across the Water* was a depiction of America's present, to the point that some mistakenly thought the "Madman" in the album's title referred to President Richard Nixon.

It had been a year since Elton had released a studio album. Not that he'd been taking a break; the interim had seen the release of the live *11-17-70* album, as well as his first soundtrack, *Friends*, not to mention that in 1971 he played over twice as many shows as he had in 1970, in eight different countries. All that traveling had provided plenty of new inspiration.

There are tales of life on the road. "Tiny Dancer" recounts Bernie's meeting his first wife and sweeping her along on their rock 'n' roll adventure. "Holiday Inn" details the boredom of touring when you're not onstage, moving from one bland hotel room to another, enlivened by Davey Johnstone's work on mandolin and sitar. Also playing acoustic guitar, it was Johnstone's first time working with Elton. Percussionist Ray Cooper, who would go on to work extensively with Elton, also made his debut appearance on one of Elton's albums with this release.

Life among the down-and-outers, those left to their own devices on America's streets, is a subject explored in "Razor

Elton and Bernie sit for a publicity shot circa 1971.

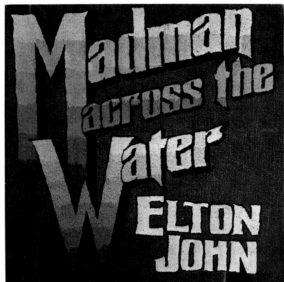

Onstage in 1971. *Madman Across the Water* was another success in the US, where it reached #8.

Face" (the homeless), and "Rotten Peaches" (the ex-cons). "Indian Sunset" was a moving piece about the modern plight of Native Americans, matched to music that swells with emotion. "All the Nasties" was a pushback against the media. The musical backing isn't entirely successful, a curious mix of plaintive singing during the verses segueing into overly lush choruses featuring a church choir. The real note of interest in this song is in the veiled references to something in Elton's life he was keeping hidden, a subtle coming-out song, as Elton later confirmed.

"Levon" and the title track are the album's most anthemic songs. Producer Gus Dudgeon said the title of the former song was a reference to The Band's Levon Helm, which Bernie later denied. But the song certainly emulates The Band's rock/folk/jazz mix. And the "Madman" in the title song appears to be in absolute thrall to his insanity, as illustrated by the dramatic music and Paul Buckmaster's swirling orchestrations. An earlier version, with Mick Ronson on lead guitar, was recorded during the *Tumbleweed* sessions and appears as a bonus track on later editions of the album.

Madman Across the Water was another success in the US, where it reached #8 (the singles "Tiny Dancer" and "Levon" reached #41 and #24, respectively). But it stalled at #41 in the UK, nor were there any accompanying hit singles. There was something of a backlash against Elton in England at the time, from those who dismissed him as a pop star who spent too much time currying favor with the Americans. It was a disappointment to Elton, who briefly wondered if he was on the right track: "I thought of quitting. I really thought I'd gone as far as I was going to."

He'd soon find a way to inject new life into his career.

15

"A ROSE BY ANY OTHER NAME"

OFFICIALLY BECOMING ELTON JOHN

JANUARY 6, 1972

Frances Gumm. Archibald Leach. Reginald Dwight. They don't quite have the same ring as Judy Garland, Cary Grant, or Elton John.

Reg Dwight believed that with a name like "Reg Dwight," he'd never be considered "pop star material." Conversely, in his Bluesology days, he had felt his bandmates had names that surely belonged on a marquee, like Stuart Brown and Pete Gavin. There was another member whose name also caught his imagination: saxophonist Elton Dean. After he'd decided to leave Bluesology, Reg asked Elton Dean if he could take his name. Dean understandably thought that was a bit much. Reg perused the other band members' names and decided a mix-and-match was in order; Elton, from Elton Dean, and John, from Long John Baldry. Hence: Elton John.

"Elton John" made his public debut with his first single, "I've Been Loving You," in 1968. But before success arrived in 1970, the people who'd been working with him still tended to call him "Reg." As "Elton John" became better known, this began to cause some problems. The breaking point came in late 1971, when Elton was shopping at London department store Fortnum and Mason. When it came time to pay, the clerk recognized him as Elton John, but refused to take his check, which still bore the name Reginald Dwight.

An irritated Elton decided to make his professional name official, filing an application to change his name by deed poll. He also decided to give himself a new middle name, Hercules, not in reference to the mythological champion of ancient Greece, but after the horse in the British TV sitcom *Steptoe and Son*.

Elton's mother was unhappy, but Elton had no regrets. Officially becoming Elton John was another step toward becoming his true self.

Elton drew on the names of Long John Baldry, former Bluesology bandmate Elton Dean (seen at top, second from right, with Keith Tippett's ensemble), and Hercules, the horse in the British TV sitcom *Steptoe and Son*.

Reg Dwight no more.
Elton at a 1972
press function.

At home with the fleet, April 1972.

"A REALLY IMPORTANT ALBUM FOR US"

HONKY CHÂTEAU

MAY 19, 1972 (UK RELEASE)

MAY 26, 1972 (US RELEASE)

For an ardent record collector such as Elton, who'd carefully noted the chart performances of records in his notebooks since childhood, it must've been a momentous occasion to have one of his own records top the charts for the first time.

And that's not the only notable thing about *Honky Château*. It marked the beginning of a new musical direction for Elton. After making minimal contributions on his previous albums, Dee Murray and drummer Nigel Olsson were finally full participants. Davey Johnstone was also now a full-time member of the band, taking up the electric guitar to relieve Elton of always playing the dominant melodies on his

piano. And it was the first time Elton recorded outside the safe, familiar studio environments of London.

Château d'Hérouville, built in 1740, was located in the village d'Hérouville, twenty-four miles from Paris. The château had a storied history, serving as a romantic destination for the couple Frédéric Chopin and George Sand. Vincent van Gogh also strolled the grounds and may have painted there. Film composer Michel Magne bought the property in 1962 and converted it into a recording facility, named Strawberry Studios, in 1969. Aside from Magne's own music, Rex Foster was the first musician to record an album at the château, *Roads of Tomorrow* (1971).

Scenes from Château d'Hérouville while recording *Honky Château* in January 1972.

"Rocket Man" on *Top of the Pops*, May 1972.

Elton chose to record outside of England for tax purposes, and when producer Gus Dudgeon, scouting likely sites in France, first looked around the property, he knew the château would provide an idyllic setting. Bernie would write in his room upstairs on his typewriter; Elton would find a newly written lyric waiting for him when he got up in the morning and finish off the song; the band would rehearse it and record the same day. It reminded Elton of the assembly line "hit factory" setup of labels like Motown, and inspiration flowed. One day, he wrote the music for "Mona Lisas and Mad Hatters," "Amy," and "Rocket Man" before the band had even come down to breakfast.

"Rocket Man" was an obvious choice for a single and would go on to be one of Elton's signature songs. The other single was "Honky Cat," which opens the album with panache, a bright, buoyant number with Elton's honky-tonk piano adding a touch of nostalgia. There's a lighthearted feeling to much of the album; even "I Think I'm Going to Kill Myself" is surprisingly breezy (probably because the teenage protagonist is only miffed that he can't use the car). Conversely, "Mona Lisas and Mad Hatters" is Bernie's bittersweet portrait of his first visit to New York City, in all its tawdry glamour. With no elaborate orchestrations or overdubs, the album has the invigorating sound of a tight rock band.

Honky Château was the first of a record seven consecutive albums that would top the US charts; it would also reach #2 in the UK. Together, Elton, Davey, Dee, and Nigel had hit upon a distinctive sound that would make them one of the biggest acts of the 70s.

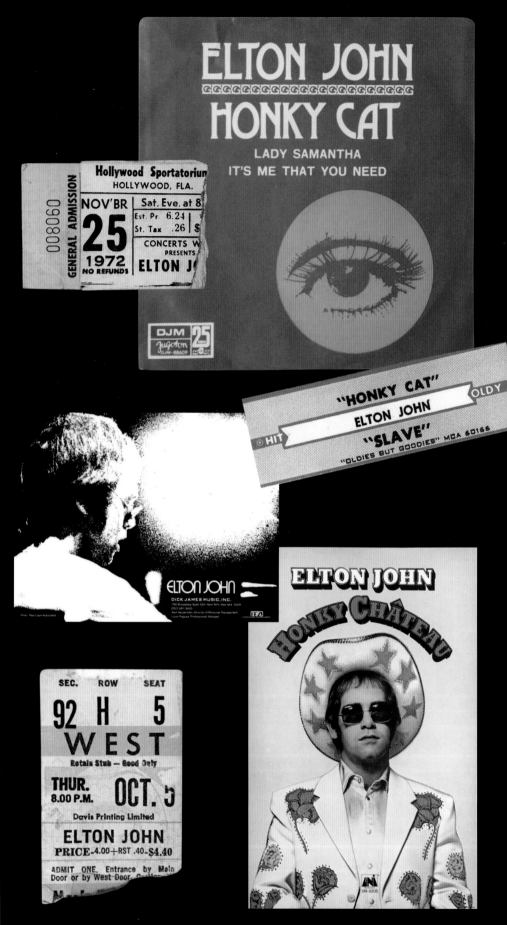

ELTON JOHN
YOUR SONG

NIGEL OLSSEN
DEE MURRAY
DAUBY JOHNSTONE

Eric Foerster

Hamburg
MUSIKHALLE
Donnerstag, 16. März 1972
20.00 Uhr

MAMA
CONCERTS
PRESENTS

Durchführung:
Konzertdirektion Karsten Jahnke,
Hamburg 11

Karten an den bekannten Vorverkaufsstellen.
Vergünstigte Karten beim Kulturring der Jugend
und in den ASTA-Theaterkassen

17

"THEY'LL NEVER KILL THE THRILLS WE GOT"

"CROCODILE ROCK"

NOVEMBER 4, 1972
(UK RELEASE)

NOVEMBER 20, 1972
(US RELEASE)

Performing at the Guildhall, Portsmouth, England, August 26, 1972.

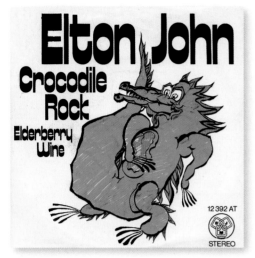

Backstage at the Royal Variety Performance at the London Palladium, October 30, 1972. From left: drummer Nigel Olsson, unknown, Elton, guitarist Davey Johnstone, and bassist Dee Murray.

It's a song Elton himself referred to as "disposable pop." But it's also the song that became his first number-one single.

"Crocodile Rock" was written as something of a lark, a fond look back at the songwriters' youth, when they were discovering the allure of rock 'n' roll. Against a backdrop of pounding piano and Farfisa organ, the singer recounts the bliss of dancing to the song with his sweetheart, Susie.

Had that been the extent of the narrative—happiness forever after, dancing to the "Crocodile Rock"—the song would indeed be little more than a trifle. But Bernie's lyric gives it a bittersweet twist, as the young lovers grow up and Susie moves on to new music, leaving the narrator with nothing but his memories.

It's the poignancy that gives the song its emotional resonance, and likely played a role in its longevity. The first single released from *Don't Shoot Me, I'm Only the Piano Player*, it topped the US charts for three weeks, gave Elton his first gold single, and reached #5 in the UK. And it quickly became a mainstay of Elton's live act, guaranteed to get the audience on their feet, singing along. With a sound that Elton saw as a send-

up of early-60s pop, and its references to Chevys, blue jeans, and "Rock Around the Clock," it also foreshadowed the 50s/60s nostalgia wave of the 1970s that encompassed such retro-themed entertainments as the film *American Graffiti*, Ringo Starr's cover of Johnny Burnette's "You're Sixteen," and the television series *Happy Days*.

"I wanted it to be a tribute to all those people I used to go and see as a kid," Elton told *Beat Instrumental* at the time. "That's why I used the Del Shannon–type vocals and that bit from Pat Boone's 'Speedy Gonzales.'" It was a reference that would cost him, as "Speedy Gonzales" songwriter Buddy Kaye filed suit, alleging that the falsetto "la-la-la" section in "Crocodile Rock" emulated

Kaye's song too closely. The suit was settled out of court.

Although it's remained one of Elton's most popular songs, it's not one he has a lot of fondness for. "It was written as a kind of a joke, like a pastiche," he told the *Mirror* in 2021. Being the consummate entertainer, he had no problem giving his audience what they wanted, and if they wanted to hear "Crocodile Rock," he'd play it for them. But once his touring days were over, he looked forward to never having to perform it again, telling the *Mirror*, "The last time I have to sing 'Crocodile Rock' I will probably throw a party."

And we really thought the "Crocodile Rock" would last.

"GRAB MYSELF A PLACE IN HISTORY"

DON'T SHOOT ME, I'M ONLY THE PIANO PLAYER

JANUARY 22, 1973
(UK RELEASE)

JANUARY 26, 1973
(US RELEASE)

Elton's sixth studio album was steeped in nostalgia for rock 'n' roll's early years, starting with its cover, depicting a 50s-era leather-jacketed youth and his teenage date buying a movie ticket (with the album's title cleverly used as the movie title on the marquee), and songs about late nights, schoolboy crushes, and dreams of stardom.

And dance crazes. A gentle parody of the era's music, "Crocodile Rock" became an instant classic. Elsewhere, the lovelorn student of "Teacher I Need You" might have "John Wayne stances" and "Errol Flynn advances," but he's still too shy to confess his love directly, the opening roiling piano illustrating his underlying anxiety. The runaway lovers of "Blues for My Baby and Me" are lulled to sleep by the steady groove of the music playing on the Greyhound's radio as they head for the coast. "I'm Going to Be a Teenage Idol," a confident rocker, was about Elton's friend Marc Bolan, the hippie sprite turned glam rocker, with whom Elton enjoyed a friendly rivalry.

But there were also songs from a more adult perspective. In "Daniel," a brother watches with sadness as his elder sibling flies off to Spain. What gives the song its enigmatic feeling is the editing Elton gave to Bernie's lyric. Bernie had been inspired by a story about a Vietnam veteran, now disabled because of the conflict, who wanted nothing more than to be left in peace. But in writing the music, Elton left out the song's final verse, which explained the story. He told one journalist he felt the verse was "too American." To another he said he simply wanted to maintain an air of mystery, and that not explaining everything made a song "more mystical." The song also led to a dispute with

Onstage with the Beach Boys at the Crystal Palace Bowl, London, June 3, 1972.

Elton's publisher, Dick James, who didn't want to release it as a single. But Elton insisted, and even paid for the advertising, on condition that he be paid back if the song was a hit. Elton won—"Daniel" reached #2 in the US, #4 in the UK.

"Elderberry Wine" is another highlight. The thumping piano intro sets you up to expect an ode to good times; instead, it's a bittersweet look back at happier days, when the song's protagonist had a good woman beside him. And the melancholy of "High Flying Bird" seems like a heartfelt plea from a former lover, but a close look at the lyrics reveals a darker story of domination and obsession.

Don't Shoot Me was Elton's first album to top both the US and UK charts. Fittingly for an album that spends much of its time looking at the past, its title was inspired by a Marx Brother. While relaxing in Malibu, California, after recording was completed, Elton was introduced to Groucho Marx by a mutual friend. The legendary comedian's rapid-fire quips (including his observation that Elton's names were in the wrong order and he should really call himself "John Elton") eventually prompted Elton to throw up his hands in defeat and proclaim, "Don't shoot me, I'm only the piano player!" It seemed the perfect name for his just-completed album, and the record cover would feature a poster of the Marx Brothers' film *Go West* as a tribute.

Don't Shoot Me combined nostalgia for bygone youth culture with songs presented from more of an adult perspective.

Performing in 1973. *Don't Shoot Me* was Elton's first album to top both the US and UK charts.

19

"A COMPANY THAT WORKS ITS BOLLOCKS OFF"

THE ROCKET RECORD COMPANY LAUNCHES

APRIL 30, 1973

Cutting loose at the Rocket Records launch party in Gloucestershire, England, April 1973.

Being an avid record collector, it's little surprise that Elton would one day own a record label—one that he launched in his own inimitable style.

While relaxing with drinks one evening during the recording of *Don't Shoot Me, I'm Only the Piano Player*, guitarist Davey Johnstone mentioned he wanted to record a solo album but hadn't been able to get a deal. To Elton, the solution seemed obvious: start a record company themselves. Arrangements were quickly made to get the venture off the ground. As Elton told UK music weekly *Disc*, "What we're offering is individual love and devotion, a fucking good royalty for the artist, and a company that works its bollocks off." The logo was a drawing of a smiling locomotive, cheerfully pulling a train over a green landscape.

The first party to launch the label was held on March 25, 1973, aboard the boat *John D*, which floated down the Thames with a guestlist that included Ringo Starr, Paul Simon, and Rod Stewart. But the next party, on April 30, upped the ante.

The two-hundred-plus invited guests took a specially chartered train from London's Paddington Station to Moreton-in-Marsh in the Cotswolds. On arrival, they were met by a brass band that escorted them to the village's town hall, where a lavish spread of food and drink awaited them. Entertainment was provided by two of the label's acts: Mike Silver and Longdancer (featuring guitarist Dave Stewart, later of Eurythmics), followed by a short set from Elton and his band.

The US wasn't left out. A third launch party was held at Universal Studios in LA. Elton played a few songs for attendees with backing vocals provided by Dusty Springfield and Nona Hendryx. There would eventually be a Rocket Records office in LA as well as London.

Rocket Records managed to land some unexpected hits. Kiki Dee (born Pauline Matthews) was a well-regarded singer who'd thus far found only limited success. She signed to Rocket after touring with Elton as a backing singer and reached #13 in the UK charts with an English-language version of the French song "Amoureuse" in 1973—the label's first hit. She'd soon find even more success with Elton.

Rocket also revived the career of Neil Sedaka, the pop singer/songwriter

who'd moved to the UK in the 1970s as his stateside career had waned. Elton was surprised that the former hit-maker had no US record deal and promptly signed him to Rocket. Sedaka subsequently had a string of Top 40 albums and singles in the States, including the #1 hits "Laughter in the Rain" and "Bad Blood" (with Elton providing backing vocals on the latter).

Rocket releases were initially distributed by MCA in the US, and Island in the UK. Elton was still under contract to DJM when Rocket started and didn't begin releasing records on the label until 1976, with the album *Blue Moves*. Rocket had other hits with artists like Judie Tzuke, the Lambrettas, and country singer Fred Wedlock ("The Oldest Swinger in Town"), but by the late 1980s the roster had slimmed down to Elton alone. No longer an active label, the name lives on in Elton's company Rocket Music Entertainment Group.

A launch party was also held at Universal Studios in LA. Elton played a few songs with backing vocals provided by Dusty Springfield and Nona Hendryx.

20

"THE GREATEST SIN IS TO BE BORING"

HOLLYWOOD BOWL EXTRAVAGANZA

SEPTEMBER 7, 1973

Even by Elton's own extravagant standards, the opening of his first Hollywood Bowl performance was over the top.

A huge illustration of Elton in top hat and tails, flanked on either side by a chorus line of young women, served as a backdrop on stage, above a large white staircase. The show's emcee was an unexpected choice: Linda Lovelace, star of the softcore porn hit *Deep Throat*. After welcoming the audience, she announced, "On this spectacular night, we hope to revive some of the glamour that has all but disappeared from show business," and introduced a series of "distinguished guests" who paraded down the steps. The Queen of England. Elvis. Frankenstein's monster. The Pope. All of them lookalikes, but festive, nonetheless. And there were more to come. All four of The Beatles. Batman and Robin. Groucho Marx. Mae West.

Finally, it was Elton's turn (the real Elton). Lovelace introduced him as "the co-star

of my next movie—the biggest, most colossal, gigantic, fantastic, Elton John!" As the Twentieth Century-Fox movie theme blared, Elton triumphantly came down the stairs in what he called his "Incredible Cheese Straw Outfit"—a white suit lavishly embellished with white marabou feathers. Accompanying his descent, the lids of the five grand pianos, each painted a different color (pink, blue, red, orange, silver), were opened one by one, their lids spelling out E-L-T-O-N. As a final flourish, four hundred doves were supposed to fly out of the pianos, but some were too stupefied by the noise to move; Elton's manager John Reid and Bernie Taupin ended up coming on stage to help, grabbing the birds and tossing them upward in an effort to get them airborne.

The crowd loved it. By then, excess was expected at an Elton John show. But it was more than simply showing off. As a performer who spent most of his time sitting behind a piano keyboard, as opposed to a lead singer who could

roam the stage, Elton had minimal opportunities to make a visual impression. Striding onstage in an elaborate getup was one way of doing so.

Audiences had watched Elton's sartorial tastes develop over the years. He started out at his US debut at the Troubadour wearing yellow overalls; by the end of the run, he was sporting silver hot pants and a T-shirt with the words "Rock and Roll" spelled out in sequins. He also picked up a gold lamé tailcoat and Mickey Mouse ears during his trip.

The sky soon became the limit, and Elton began working with costume designers to make personally tailored, evermore fabulous creations. Accessorized appropriately, of course. One could never have too many hats. Or use too many feathers. There were specially designed eyeglasses as well, with lights that spelled out E-L-T-O-N or ZOOM (though he found them so heavy, they pinched his nose).

Elton admitted that Bernie wasn't keen on the elaborate costumes, finding them a distraction. Critics, too, felt his penchant for flamboyance was occasionally in danger of eclipsing his musical skills. But Elton was unrepentant. "I thought I was forging myself into a personality that was like nobody else in rock." And so he did.

Hollywood Bowl, September 7, 1973. Elton's "Incredible Cheese Straw Outfit" was a white suit lavishly embellished with marabou feathers.

21

•••••••••••••••••••••••

THE LATE-NIGHT, DOUBLE-FEATURE PICTURE SHOW

•••••••••••••••••••••••

GOODBYE YELLOW BRICK ROAD

•••••••••••••••••••••••

OCTOBER 5, 1973
(US AND UK RELEASE)

Elton hadn't intended to make a double album. But the songs just kept coming. In the end, it was decided there was too much good material to slim down to one record. And so *Goodbye Yellow Brick Road* became Elton's only two-LP studio release—and, aside from greatest hits compilations and soundtracks, his bestselling album.

The sessions got off to a bumpy start. With Château d'Hérouville unavailable, Elton opted to record at Dynamic Sound Studios in Jamaica, where the Rolling Stones had partially recorded *Goats Head Soup*. But on arriving, they found the studio in poor condition; cockroaches scuttled out of the piano when Elton played it, and the music they recorded sounded terrible when played back. By the time the decision was made to leave, Château d'Hérouville had become available, so the musicians reconvened in France.

One benefit of the Jamaican sojourn was that Elton had largely spent his time in his room writing songs, so most of the material was completed by the time sessions continued at the Château. The album would feature four of Elton's best-loved songs, all of them released as singles. "Saturday Night's Alright for Fighting" is one of the few out-and-out rockers that Elton's ever recorded, with Jerry Lee Lewis an obvious influence. Reaching #12 US, #7 UK, it's a rousing number that inevitably gets the crowd on their feet when played live. "Candle in the Wind" was a tribute to Marilyn Monroe and the destructive power of fame; this initial version of the song reached #11 in the UK and was not released in the US.

"Bennie and the Jets" also wasn't initially planned for US release. It's a taut, almost stark piece that's as much a critique of the music business as it is a

The Christmas show at the Hammersmith Odeon, London, December 21, 1973.

The Christmas show at the Hammersmith
Odeon, London, December 21, 1973.

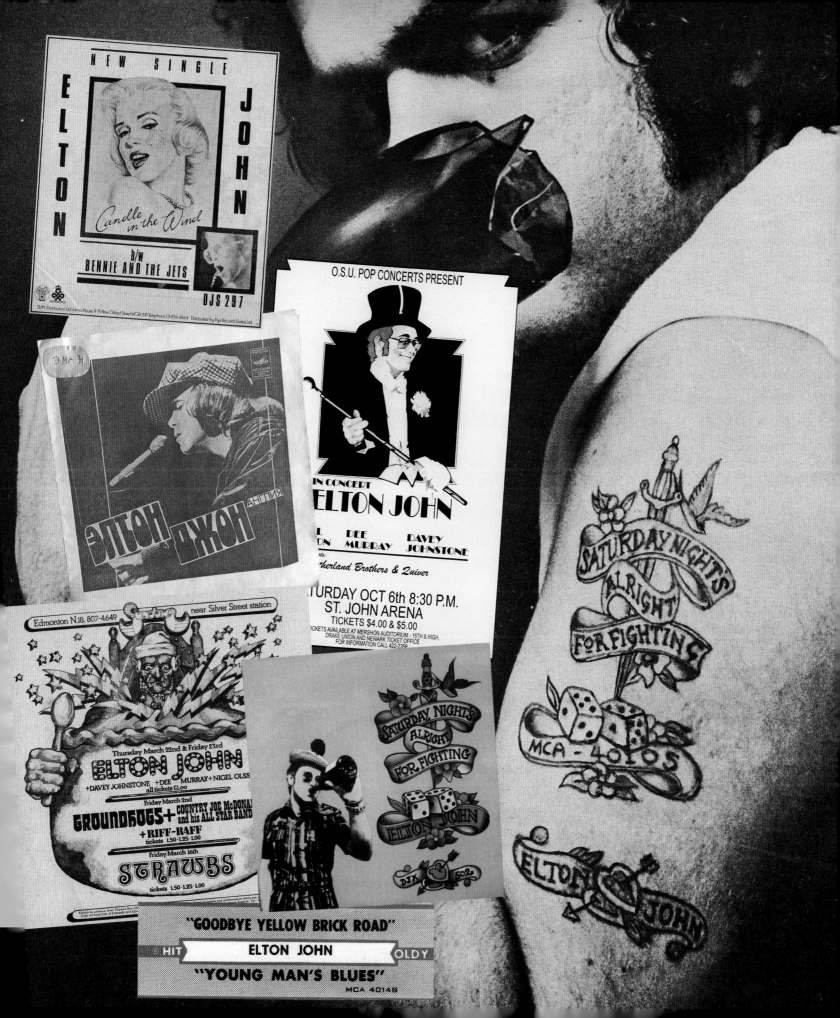

University of Georgia's Stegeman Coliseum,
Athens, Georgia, October 25, 1973.

Stepping out from behind the keys for a 1973 television appearance.

fan's ecstatic response to the weird and wonderful Bennie in her electric boots. After becoming a surprise favorite on Detroit R&B radio station WJLB, it was released as a single and topped the charts (it also became Elton's first Top 40 hit in *Billboard*'s Soul Singles chart). In the UK, the song appeared only as the B-side of "Candle."

And then there's the title track. *Silent Movies, Talking Pictures* had been discarded as an album title, but "Goodbye Yellow Brick Road" (which reached #2 US, #6 UK) kept the movie theme idea that runs throughout the album intact. Though, ironically, while the haunting song has the protagonist

bidding farewell to high society in favor of a simpler life, the iconic cover art shows Elton not leaving, but stepping onto the yellow brick road, sporting the satin jacket that was *de rigueur* for 70s rockers and wearing red platforms in place of ruby slippers.

Marilyn's cinematic dreams aren't the only ones unspooling on the album; "Roy Rogers" puts in an appearance, while "The Ballad of Danny Bailey (1909–34)" could be the title of one of Bernie's beloved westerns (it's actually about bootleggers in Kentucky), and "All the Girls Love Alice" updates the lesbian angst of *The Killing of Sister George*. And at the urging of his producer, Elton

created one of his finest instrumentals, "Funeral for a Friend," which provides a striking opening for the album, especially as it segues into another furious rocker, "Love Lies Bleeding."

The album topped the charts on both sides of the Atlantic, sold in excess of thirty million copies, and is widely considered the high-water mark of Elton's career.

Sporting a new Ralph Nudie suit on
Top of the Pops, 1973.

22

UP CLOSE AND PERSONAL

ELTON JOHN & BERNIE TAUPIN SAY GOODBYE NORMA JEAN AND OTHER THINGS

DECEMBER 4, 1973
(UK BROADCAST)

MAY 12, 1974
(US BROADCAST)

As one of the first documentaries about him, *Elton John & Bernie Taupin* provides an entertaining look at Elton at his 1970s peak.

Elton had met the film's director, Bryan Forbes, when he and John Reid moved outside of London to Virginia Water, Surrey, in 1972. Forbes lived in the area and owned a bookshop in town. When Elton first visited, Forbes mistook him for one of the Bee Gees. Elton became good friends with Forbes and his wife, actress Nanette Newman, and loved visiting their home, where one might encounter any number of well-known actors and maybe even the odd royal or two.

In addition to directing and producing the documentary, Forbes provides droll commentary. "Elton John plays cricket as he plays the piano; dressed to kill, and as if his life depended upon it. . . . At twenty-six, he walks on five-foot heels where lesser angels fear to tread." His friendship with Elton brings a relaxed intimacy to their in-person encounters, Forbes casually sprawling in a chair as he watches Elton play the piano.

After the expected questions about Elton's childhood and meeting Bernie,

the interviews become more insightful. There's an undercurrent of insecurity: Elton saying he could never be a classical musician because of his "midget boxer's hands," and answering the question about where he thinks he'll be in twenty-five years with the reply "Bald, actually!" (one of a number of references he makes to his thinning hair and his weight). When Forbes asks him about his tendency to send himself up in interviews, Elton explains it's because

Elton and Bernie in 1974, around the time of the US broadcast.

he doesn't want to come across as too much of a goody-goody; asked about his vices, he only admits to collecting.

In contrast to the elaborately costumed performer we see in the live sequences, the offstage Elton is thoughtful about his career, as when he points out that while he appeared to be an overnight success, he'd been a professional musician for six years before his breakthrough. Already having numerous hits to his name, he says he still thinks his best work is yet to come: "I don't think I've matured enough."

The live footage was shot at Elton's 1973 Hollywood Bowl appearance.

He compares building a setlist to having sex ("You just try and keep the best bit until the end"), and, interestingly, says he doesn't think anything when he walks out on stage: "My mind's a complete blank. I don't feel anything, I don't feel anything at all."

Bernie is the only other person interviewed to any extent. "He writes as he feels, when he feels," Forbes observes. "Self-isolated in a nostalgic ivory tower, inhabited by yesterday's heroes, and surrounded by the golden discs that signify that nostalgia has its rewards." There's also footage of Elton and the band at Château d'Hérouville ("It's indeed odd to find tomorrow's

music being made in yesterday's crumbling splendor"), working on *Goodbye Yellow Brick Road* and strolling the grounds.

Interestingly, considering the prominence it would come to attain, a lot of time is spent on discussing "Candle in the Wind," Bernie explaining his fascination for Marilyn Monroe, and Elton seen recording the song.

Though a short documentary, it has a decided charm, most notably due to the absence of today's rapid-style editing. The 2014 box set edition of *Goodbye Yellow Brick Road* included the program on DVD.

Photo used to promote 1974 US broadcast.

ROCKY MOUNTAIN HIGH

CARIBOU

JUNE 24, 1974 (US RELEASE)

JUNE 28, 1974 (UK RELEASE)

Elton's band poses for a portrait in an alpine setting. From left: Nigel Olsson, Davey Johnstone, Dee Murray, and Ray Cooper.

Producer Gus Dudgeon dismissed the album as a "piece of crap." Elton himself said the songs had an element of "coasting." As he told author Tom Doyle, "When you're at number one, you can do anything you want." But the John/Taupin team was still on a hot streak, and *Caribou* was yet another chart-topping album, and going double platinum to boot.

The sessions marked the first time Elton had recorded in the US. Caribou Ranch was an isolated studio near Nederland, Colorado, forty-five miles from Denver and over eight thousand feet above sea level. The studio was owned by Jim Guercio, who managed and produced the band Chicago, as well as producing numerous other acts, such as Blood, Sweat & Tears and surrealistic comedy group the Firesign Theater.

Wedding bells
for Elton and
Renate Blauel

1984
FEBRUARY 14

40

Watford
Football Club
at the FA Cup
Final

1984
MAY 19

41

Live Aid feeds
Africa

1985
JULY 13

42

Marooned on
*Desert Island
Discs*

1986
JUNE 1

43

Elton goes
classic

1986
DECEMBER 14

44

Elton's epic
garage sale

1988
SEPTEMBER 6–9

45

Taking
Sun
win

19
DECEM

46

PART

The Elton John
AIDS Foundation
Oscar party

1993
MARCH 29

53

Inducted into the
RRHOF

1994
JANUARY 19

54

The Lion King gets
the royal treatment

1994
JUNE 12

55

"Face to Face" with
Billy Joel

1994
JULY 8–AUGUST 21

56

Throwing tantrums,
catching tiaras

1996
JULY 7

57

Rewriting "Candle
in the Wind" for
Princess Diana

1997
SEPTEMBER 6

58

Elton
Knigh

19
FEBRU

59

Elton guests with
Kate Bush
(among others)

2011
NOVEMBER 21

66

God save
the Queen's
Diamond
Jubilee
concert

2012
JUNE 4

67

Pnau gives
Elton a remix
on *Good
Morning to
the Night*

2012
JULY 16

68

Wedding bells
for Elton and
David Furnish

2014
DECEMBER 21

69

Going for a
spin with
James Corden
in *Carpool
Karaoke*

2016
FEBRUARY 7

70

Rocketman
gives Elton
the biopic
treatment

2019
MAY 16

71

El
autobi

20
OCTOE

72

Loving
n's first
ingle

A full album at
last: *Empty Sky*

1969
JUNE 6

8

Release of
Elton John

1970
APRIL 10

9

The first classic
single: "Your Song"

1970
OCTOBER 26

10

US breakthrough at
LA's Troubadour club

1970
AUGUST 25–30

11

The tumblin'
*Tumbleweed
Connection*

1970
OCTOBER 30

12

11-17-70: the
first live album

1971
APRIL 1

13

---

out all
s at the
d Bowl

73
BER 7

A trip through
the Land of Oz:
*Goodbye
Yellow Brick
Road*

1973
OCTOBER

21

Elton and
Bernie's Q&A in
the Bryan
Forbes
documentary

1974
MAY 12

22

Caribou, the
first studio
album recorded
in the US

1974
JUNE 24

23

The very first
Greatest Hits
collection

1974
NOVEMBER 4

24

Happy
Thanksgiving
with John
Lennon

1974
NOVEMBER 28

25

"He's a pinball
wizard"

1975
MARCH 18

26

3: CHANGE IT UP TO SHAKE IT UP

ng in at
ditch
ege

77
17

Elton meets
the Muppets

1978
JANUARY 8

34

Elton swaps in
Gary Osborne
on *A Single
Man*

1978
OCTOBER

35

Finding his
inner soul man
on "Mama
Can't Buy You
Love"

1979
JUNE

36

Back in the
USSR

1979
MAY 21–28

37

Meeting the
masses in
Central Park

1980
SEPTEMBER 13

38

Back with
Bernie on *Too
Low for Zero*

1983
MAY 23

39

PART 1: CHASING THE DREAM

Reginald Kenneth Dwight is born

1947
MARCH 25

1

Elton discovers Elvis

1956
SPRING

2

"Come Back Baby," Elton's first single release

1965
JULY 23

3

An *NME* ad brings Elton and Bernie together

1967
JUNE 17

4

Elton's session work on Tom Jones' "Delilah"

1968
FEBRUARY

5

False start; the *Regimental Sgt. Zippo* album

1967-1968

6

"I've Bee[n] You," Elto[n's] solo s[ingle]

19[68]
MAR[CH]

7

Life on the road in *Madman Across the Water*

1971
NOVEMBER

14

From Reginald Dwight to Elton Hercules John

1972
JANUARY 6

15

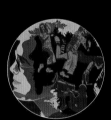

Le *Honky Château* s'il vous plaît

1972
MAY 19

16

"I remember when rock was young"

1972
NOVEMBER 4

17

Tickling the ivories: . . . *I'm Only the Piano Player*

1973
JANUARY 22

18

The Rocket Record Company opening party

1973
APRIL 30

19

Pulling [out] the stop[s in] Hollywo[od]

19[73]
SEPTEM[BER]

20

PART [2]

Getting down on *Soul Train*

1975
MAY 17

27

The autobiographical album: *Captain Fantastic . . .*

1975
MAY 19

28

The last Caribou Ranch roundup: *Rock of the Westies*

1975
OCTOBER 4

29

The extravaganza of Elton John Week

1975
OCTOBER 20–26

30

"Don't Go Breaking My Heart" tops the UK chart

1976
JUNE 21

31

Elton to *RS*: "I think everybody's bisexual"

1976
OCTOBER 7

32

Droppi[ng] *Shore[...]* *Col[...]*

19[...]
JUNE

33

Getting clean
and sober

*Sleeping with
the Past* takes
Elton back to
the top

"Sacrifice:"
Elton's first
solo UK
chart topper

1990
AUGUST 10

49

The first Elton
and Bernie
tribute album

Elton and
George Michael's
big hit single

Honoring Freddie
Mercury

on *The
—and
ning

88
BER 12

1989
AUGUST

47

1990
MAY

48

1991
OCTOBER 22

50

1991
NOVEMBER 25

51

1992
APRIL 20

52

5: NATIONAL TREASURE

gets a
thood

"Rocket Man"
serenades a
Space Shuttle
launch

After 30 years,
"Tiny Dancer"
finds fame

The Red Piano
opens in Vegas

Billy Elliott
gets his dance
shoes on

A birthday party
to remember

Elton teams with
Leon Russell on
The Union

98
ARY 24

1998
OCTOBER 29

60

2000
SEPTEMBER 8

61

2004
FEBRUARY 13

62

2005
MAY 11

63

2007
MARCH 25

64

2010
OCTOBER 19

65

A *Jewel
Box* full of
rarities

Making music
through
COVID-19: *The
Lockdown
Sessions*

The long
goodbye: the
*Farewell Yellow
Brick Road*
tour

ton's
ography:
Me

2020
NOVEMBER 13

73

919
BER 15

2021
OCTOBER 22

74

2023
JULY 8

75

Producer Gus Dudgeon dismissed the album as a "piece of crap." Elton himself said the songs had an element of "coasting." As he told author Tom Doyle, "When you're at number one, you can do anything you want." But the John/Taupin team was still on a hot streak, and *Caribou* was yet another chart-topping album, and going double platinum to boot.

The sessions marked the first time Elton had recorded in the US. Caribou Ranch was an isolated studio near Nederland, Colorado, forty-five miles from Denver and over eight thousand feet above sea level. The studio was owned by Jim Guercio, who managed and produced the band Chicago, as well as producing numerous other acts, such as Blood, Sweat & Tears and surrealistic comedy group the Firesign Theater.

Elton had liked the records he'd heard recorded at the studio by Rick Derringer and Joe Walsh. But his own sessions were rushed. Elton, Bernie, and the band arrived there (Elton slept in a cabin with a bed previously owned by President Grover Cleveland) in January

1974. Recording had to be done quickly, as a new tour was scheduled to start in February; depending on the source, by the time they arrived, there were only eight to ten days to complete the album.

And they ended up having even less time than that. After writing the songs, Elton's mood swings got the better of him and it took him three days to unwind so recording could finally begin. His anxiety wasn't helped by everyone's copious drug use; "It was in the winter and we always used to say there was more snow inside than outside," Bernie joked to Doyle.

But the album does have its highlights, beginning with the opening track, "The Bitch Is Back." The "bitch" in question was Elton himself; the phrase was a joking observation by Bernie's then-wife Maxine about his occasional grumpiness. Elton, who never hesitated to poke fun at himself, dug into the song with relish; the horn section from Tower of Power provides additional pizzazz. Released as a single, it reached #4 US (despite the reluctance of some DJs to play it, due to its perceived vulgarity) and #14 UK.

Caribou's other leading contender is the superlative ballad "Don't Let the Sun Go Down on Me" (#2 UK, #16 UK). Contrast that with the trifle that is "Solar Prestige a Gammon," whose nonsensical lyrics were a pushback to those who over-analyzed Taupin's writing (its Italian-style melody and Elton's operatic singing make it a distant cousin to the opera section of Queen's "Bohemian Rhapsody").

What Elton called the album's "uneven" quality can be jarring. *Caribou*'s sometimes giddy spirits are brought down to earth by the chilling closer, "Ticking," the sad saga of a mass killer. Elsewhere you'll find "Grimsby," an ode to an undistinguished English town; musing about UFOs in "I've Seen the Saucers"; and "Stinker," a dirty blues (which was also briefly considered as the album's title).

Though the recording of *Caribou* might not have been entirely satisfactory, Elton was happy enough with the studio that he returned to Caribou Ranch to record his next two albums.

24

ALL KILLER, NO FILLER

GREATEST HITS

NOVEMBER 4, 1974
(UK RELEASE)

NOVEMBER 8, 1974
(US RELEASE)

What's a rocker without a Halliburton case full of spectacles? September 1974.

He's released a lot more hits since 1974. And he's released numerous "best of" compilations, but Elton's *Greatest Hits*, released in November 1974, remains the bestselling of such packages, having sold over twenty-four million copies worldwide.

Elton was on a roll at the time, in the midst of a streak of six consecutive #1 studio albums, from *Honky Château* to *Rock of the Westies*. *Greatest Hits* would add another number to that.

Coming between *Caribou* and *Captain Fantastic and the Brown Dirt Cowboy*, *Greatest Hits* was a concise summary of the Elton John Story So Far.

It's a short album by today's standards— a mere ten tracks over forty-four minutes, given the constraints of vinyl. But it's the very definition of an album that's "all killer, no filler." Every song had reached a Top 10 chart, though not necessarily always in the US or UK. "Honky Cat" only reached #31 in the UK, for example. "Border Song" didn't make the Top 40 in either country (though it did so in Canada and the Netherlands). There were slightly different track listings as well. "Bennie and the Jets" was only on the US and Canadian versions of the album; on UK and Australian editions it was replaced by "Candle in the Wind."

Elton's the picture of quiet confidence on the cover, seated before his piano in a gleaming white suit, oversized sunglasses, and broad-brimmed hat, right hand on his chin, gazing directly into the camera. On its release, the album topped the US charts for ten weeks (and became his first album to sell over ten million copies in the States) and UK charts for eleven weeks. And though all the tracks were elsewhere available on Elton's studio albums, it remained a steady seller. Expanded editions followed. The 1992 reissue of the album on CD included both "Bennie and the Jets" and "Candle in the Wind." A 1996 Japanese edition dropped "Bennie and the Jets" but added "Skyline Pigeon," "Take Me to the Pilot," "Rock and Roll Madonna," "Don't Go Breaking My Heart," and "It's Me That You Need."

By then, other greatest hits collections had appeared, beginning with the obviously titled follow-ups, *Elton John's Greatest Hits Volume II* (1977) and *Elton John's Greatest Hits Volume III* (1987). *Diamonds* (2017) is the most comprehensive collection of Elton's chart successes, especially the three-CD edition.

With all the songs now available on other collections or via download, the original *Greatest Hits* is out of print. But for longtime fans, especially those who were introduced to Elton's work through this album, this ten-track slice of black vinyl will always have a nostalgic pull.

25

Japanese pressings of Elton's "Lucy in the Sky" and Lennon's "Whatever Gets You Thru the Night."

"IT FELT LIKE I'D KNOWN HIM MY ENTIRE LIFE"

A BEATLE IN THE GARDEN

NOVEMBER 28, 1974

Some people had heard rumors about what might happen at Elton's Thanksgiving Day concert at Madison Square Garden, but most were taken by surprise when, midway through the show, he announced: "Seeing as it's Thanksgiving, and Thanksgivings are joyous occasions, we thought we'd make tonight a little bit of a joyous occasion by inviting someone up with us on the stage. I'm sure he'll be no stranger to any of us, when I say it's our great privilege and your great privilege to see and hear—Mr. John Lennon!" The response was deafening. Elton later said he'd never heard an ovation that loud.

Elton had met the former Beatle in 1973 at Capitol Records' LA headquarters, when John was promoting his latest album, *Mind Games*. They took an instant liking to each other. Elton made sure to get together with his new pal whenever he visited the States.

On July 31, 1974, Elton joined Lennon in the studio when he was working on his next album, *Walls and Bridges*. Elton ended up playing piano and providing backing vocals for "Whatever Gets You Thru the Night," telling John that the bright, upbeat track was sure to be a hit. When Lennon demurred, Elton threw

The 1981 EP featuring three tracks.

down a challenge: If the song reached #1, Lennon would join Elton to perform the number on stage. Convinced it would never happen, Lennon agreed.

The following month, Lennon flew to the Caribou Ranch in Colorado to return the favor, playing guitar and singing backing vocals on Elton's cover of John's "Lucy in the Sky with Diamonds," giving the song a reggae lilt in the chorus. "Whatever Gets You Thru the Night" was released as a single in September, with "Lucy in the Sky with Diamonds" following in November. Both tracks topped the US charts, and Elton called on Lennon to honor his bet.

They naturally performed their two hits. Then a nervous Lennon, joking that he wanted to get off the stage so he could be sick, introduced the final number, as being "by an old, estranged fiancé of mine named Paul": The Beatles' rocker "I Saw Her Standing There." Lennon returned to the stage during the encore to sing along to "The Bitch Is Back." It was Lennon's penultimate live performance. The next year, his wife Yoko Ono gave birth to their son, Sean, on October 9, Lennon's birthday; Elton was named Sean's godfather.

Elton was in Australia when he heard the devastating news of Lennon's

murder on December 8, 1980; it was a loss he said he never got over. Three Elton-related tribute releases followed: three songs from the Thanksgiving show were released on an EP in 1981 (and subsequently on the 1990 *Lennon* box set and reissued versions of Elton's *Here and There*). Best known is the John/Taupin number "Empty Garden (Hey Hey Johnny)," which appeared on *Jump Up!* (1982). Elton also wrote a melancholy, largely instrumental song called "The Man Who Never Died," released in 1985 as the B-side to "Nikita."

Elton with John Lennon, Madison Square Garden, New York City, November 28, 1974.

26

"I JUST HANDED MY PINBALL CROWN TO HIM"

TOMMY

MARCH 18, 1975 (WORLD PREMIERE)

Elton with his special keyboard-equipped pinball machine.

Elton's first film appearance was one of the most memorable in any rock movie: his star turn as the "Pinball Wizard" in Ken Russell's over-the-top screen adaptation of The Who's rock opera *Tommy*.

Tommy was the band's fourth studio album, a double LP that tells the story of Tommy Walker. Rendered blind, deaf, and mute by childhood trauma, he overcomes his disabilities and becomes a charismatic leader. Following its release in May 1969, The Who performed the album in its near-entirety on tour. The first stage production not featuring the band debuted in 1971 in Seattle; a concert

rendition with the London Symphony Orchestra followed the next year. Two decades later, *The Who's Tommy* opened on Broadway in 1993.

In 1975, maverick film director Ken Russell released a typically gaudy, over-the-top, film version, its cast a mix of Hollywood and rock 'n' roll stars (Ann-Margret, Jack Nicholson, Eric Clapton, Tina Turner). Who lead singer Roger Daltrey played the title character.

When first approached to appear in the movie, Elton turned the opportunity down as his schedule was too busy (it wasn't his first film offer; director Hal

After filming, Elton kept his four-and-a-half-foot Doc Martens.

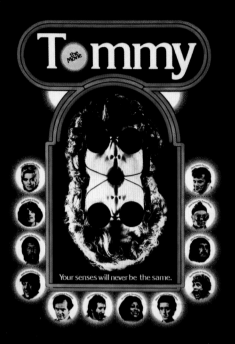

Tommy
the movie

Your senses will never be the same.

See **ELTON JOHN** starring in new
Capt. Fantastic
AND THE BROWN DIRT COWBOY
Bally 4-PLAYER FLIPPER CONVERTIBLE TO ADD-A-BALL

ELTON JOHN STYLING
International fame of **ELTON JOHN**, rock super-star, and brilliant Elton John styling with **sparkling mirror lines** on backglass gets immediate attention on location, fast, fascinating action holds play for long runs and super-star collections.

See other side for **FEATURE-GRAM** ⟶
©BALLY MFG. CORP. 1976

Real life imitates fiction—in 1976 Captain Fantastic scored a licensing deal with pinball manufacturer Bally.

Ashby had offered Elton the role of Harold in the black comedy *Harold and Maude*). Rod Stewart, who appeared in the London Symphony Orchestra version as the Pinball Wizard, was asked to reprise the role in the film. Elton reminded him that he hadn't enjoyed the LSO production and told him to turn it down. Then The Who's Pete Townshend approached Elton again and finally convinced him to take the part (to Stewart's consternation).

Elton truly made the song "Pinball Wizard" his own. He recorded with his own band, not The Who (though The Who mime to the song in the film), and came up with a spine-tingling piano intro. In the movie he towers precariously over a pinball tournament in a packed theater while wearing a pair of four-and-a-half-foot-high Doc Martens boots (which he later took home with him). As such, he was afraid to move too much, but his performance is hardly static. He attacks the piano attached to the front of his pinball table,

throws his arms up in dismay as Tommy racks up points, glares through oversized spectacles at the hotshot kid who's taking away his crown, and finally falls into the baying crowd.

The song was released only as a promotional single in the US in 1975, though it did get considerable radio airplay. In the UK, the single was officially released in May 1976, reaching #7. It's the only cover of a Who song to hit the Top 10.

Elton made "Pinball Wizard" his own, recording with his own band and coming up with a spine-tingling piano intro.

27

"I WATCH IT EVERY WEEK, AND THE WHOLE BAND WATCHES IT"

SOUL TRAIN

MAY 17, 1975
(US BROADCAST)

Soul Train episode 141.

One of Elton's proudest accomplishments in the 1970s was when he became one of the first white performers to appear on *Soul Train*.

Funk Brothers guitarist Dennis Coffey and Canadian singer Gino Vannelli had preceded Elton (Coffey in January 1972, Vannelli in February 1975), but Elton was certainly the first *major* white performer to appear. The invitation had been extended when "Philadelphia

Freedom" became a Top 40 hit on what was then *Billboard*'s Soul Singles chart (now R&B/Hip-Hop Songs). Elton didn't hesitate to accept.

After admiring Elton's glass piano and pretending he didn't know the right way to sit on its bench, smooth-voiced host Don Cornelius got serious, introducing Elton as "a very, very gifted young man, who has combined absolute genius as a musician-songwriter with a sort of

television." After a few questions from the audience (oddly, he claimed to have only been singing "for about five or six years," conveniently overlooking his years playing at the Northwood Hills Hotel and with Bluesology), he took his seat at the piano to perform "Philadelphia Freedom." The breezy number quickly got the studio audience dancing around him, as he sang a live vocal to a backing track.

He returned in a dark gray suit and matching hat (*sans* feathers) to perform "Bennie and the Jets," his first Top 40 hit in the Soul Singles chart. With its steady, slower tempo, the dancers weren't quite as energetic, but by the end they had managed to work in a few good gyrations.

It's one of Elton's most engaging television performances because he's relaxed and seems right at home. It's also notable as one of the few performances Elton gave during a year which only saw twenty-two concerts—the fewest he'd performed in a year since 1970.

psychedelic outlook on life that causes everybody that comes near to him to have a lot of fun, besides being thoroughly entertained." Elton strode on in a brown pinstripe suit, red shirt, and black fedora adorned with feathers, causing Cornelius to exclaim, "Where'd you get that *suit*, brother?" "Sears and Roebuck!" was Elton's perfectly timed response.

He then affirmed his love of *Soul Train*, calling it "the only thing you can look forward to on a tour, apart from the sports programs, on American

"Philadelphia Freedom" became a Top 40 hit on what was then Billboard's "Soul Singles" chart.

28

"THOSE DAYS WERE THE INNOCENT DAYS"

CAPTAIN FANTASTIC AND THE BROWN DIRT COWBOY

MAY 19, 1975 (US RELEASE)

MAY 23, 1975 (UK RELEASE)

Mid Summer Music, Wembley Stadium, London, June 21, 1975.

It's better than an oral history. It's Elton's and Bernie's own account of their early years together, told over the course of an album.

In looking back at the days when they hustled for work and wondered if they'd ever catch a break, Bernie created two fanciful alter egos for themselves. The flamboyant Elton was of course Captain Fantastic; Bernie, with his love of all things western, was the Brown Dirt Cowboy. Bernie described the experience of writing the lyrics as cathartic, that once he'd written the first line, the songs simply flowed out. Elton composed the melodies while traveling on the SS *France* from England to the US, serving

as an escort for John Lennon's ex-wife Cynthia and their son Julian, who was being taken to see his father. "It felt so good to be writing songs that I not only understood the lyrics to, but was a complete part of. Before, I was singing stuff that perhaps didn't relate directly to me," Elton said. Remarkably, he had to memorize the melodies he wrote aboard ship, as he didn't have a tape recorder.

Bernie had written the lyrics chronologically, and the songs were recorded chronologically as well. They also gave themselves more time to record, so the album wouldn't be another rush job like *Caribou*. The stage is set with the title song, which opens

the album, the country music at the beginning evolving into a more driving rock beat by the chorus, as Elton recalls their days of cornflakes and chocolate biscuits. Two songs in particular speak to the album's emotional core. "We All Fall in Love Sometimes," set to a delicate musical backing, is about the bond that forms between two people struggling through the same circumstances, in this case, the love between Elton and Bernie, whom Elton frequently describes as the big brother he never had. It's a song that Elton says still moves him to tears.

"Someone Saved My Life Tonight" is a stirring ballad, whose dark backstory wasn't known for some years. It references the time when Elton was briefly engaged to a woman in the 1960s, which so distressed him it led to a half-hearted suicide attempt. The "someone" who saved Elton's life was his former bandmate Long John Baldry, who advised Elton to end his engagement, enabling him to escape being "roped and tied" by the sinister princess who sits atop an electric chair. The only single released from the album, it reached #4 US, #22 UK.

It's a concept album that beautifully depicts a youthful period of hard work and hopeful dreams. The cover art, by

Alan Aldridge, was like a mashup of Ian Beck's illustration for the *Goodbye Yellow Brick Road* cover and Hieronymus Bosch.

Captain Fantastic became the first ever album to enter the US charts at #1 (it reached #2 in the UK). Elton and Bernie considered it one of their finest works, and producer Gus Dudgeon concurred: "There's not one song on there that is less than incredible."

A sequel to the album, *The Captain & the Kid*, was released in 2006.

In the Netherlands to promote *Captain Fantastic*, 1975.

29

"A LITTLE BIT MORE RAUCOUS"

ROCK OF THE WESTIES

OCTOBER 4, 1975
(UK RELEASE)

OCTOBER 20, 1975
(US RELEASE)

London, 1975. Rock of the Westies was recorded amid a hard-partying atmosphere at Caribou Ranch.

Rock of the Westies was a transitional album, with a change in musical direction largely due to the new lineup of musicians Elton was working with.

Despite the success of *Captain Fantastic*, after its recording, Elton decided to drop Dee Murray and Nigel Olsson from the band. He wasn't dissatisfied with their playing, but, always with an eye on the future, felt in need of a change (which made it ironic that he then brought in Caleb Quaye and Roger Pope, who'd played on his pre–*Honky Château* albums). Davey Johnstone, and percussionist Ray Cooper, who joined Elton on the *Madman* album, stayed in the fold for the moment.

Though the sessions were again held in the familiar setting of Caribou Ranch, there were some new tensions. Bernie's marriage was in disarray, his wife having taken up with Elton's new bass player, Kenny Passarelli. Drug use by everyone was rampant to the point of abuse. Bernie later wryly observed to *Music Connection*, "Luckily, we're all still alive to tell the tale." The song "Grow Some Funk of Your Own" was even co-written with Johnstone while he was tripping on acid.

"Grow Some Funk" was indicative of the harder-edged, funkier groove that Elton wanted to pursue. As Bernie has pointed

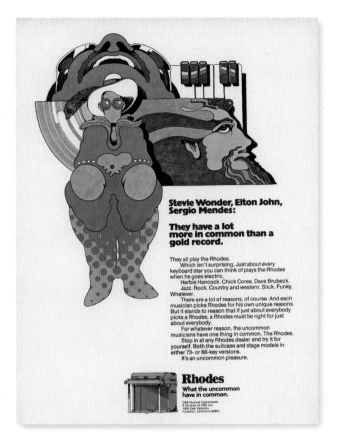

Stevie Wonder, Elton John, Sergio Mendes:

They have a lot more in common than a gold record.

They all play the Rhodes.
    Which isn't surprising. Just about every keyboard star you can think of plays the Rhodes when he goes electric.
    Herbie Hancock. Chick Corea. Dave Brubeck. Jazz. Rock. Country and western. Slick. Funky. Whatever.
    There are a lot of reasons, of course. And each musician picks Rhodes for his own unique reasons. But it stands to reason that if just about everybody picks a Rhodes, a Rhodes must be right for just about everybody.
    For whatever reason, the uncommon musicians have one thing in common. The Rhodes.
    Stop in at any Rhodes dealer and try it for yourself. Both the suitcase and stage models in either 73- or 88-key versions.
    It's an uncommon pleasure.

Rhodes
What the uncommon have in common.

CBS Musical Instruments
A Division of CBS Inc.
1300 East Valencia
Fullerton, California 92631

out, there's a brash, punk feeling to the record, a raw quality quite unlike that found on any of Elton's other albums. This is abundantly clear from the opening track, "Medley: 'Yell Help'/'Wednesday Night'/'Ugly'" (also co-written with Johnstone), a stomping rock song enlivened with backing vocals by soul trio Labelle. "Street Kids" is a swaggering number about young toughs looking for trouble (though the atmosphere is more *West Side Story* than *A Clockwork Orange*). "Dan Dare (Pilot of the Future)" cuts a steady groove in its fond farewell to the British comic book hero of the 1950s. "Billy Bones and the White Bird" has the lyrics of a sea shanty but the propulsive rhythmic beats of Bo Diddley. At the other end of the musical spectrum, the ballad "I Feel Like a Bullet (in the Gun of Robert Ford)" uses an unusual metaphor (Robert Ford was the killer of Jesse James) in its depiction of a failing relationship.

Though Elton had pushed for "Dan Dare" to be a single, the first track pulled from the album was "Island Girl"; it reached #1 US, #14 UK, though it's unlikely such a jaunty number about a Jamaican prostitute working the streets of the Big Apple would see release today. "Grow Some Funk" did less well as a single, reaching #14 US and not even cracking the UK Top 40.

The album's title is a playful reworking of the phrase "West of the Rockies." Another title considered, perhaps referring to the hard-partying atmosphere, was *Bottled and Brained* (a line from "Street Kids").

Like *Captain Fantastic*, *Rock of the Westies* entered the *Billboard* charts at #1, while reaching #5 in the UK. It was also the last in Elton's astonishing run of #1 albums in the US and the last time he recorded at Caribou Ranch, marking the end of a prolific era in his career.

30

"THE VERY BIGGEST THING TO HIT LA IN AGES"

ELTON JOHN WEEK

OCTOBER 20–26, 1975

Dodger Stadium, Los Angeles, October 25–26, 1975.

At the height of Elton's popularity in the 1970s, Elton John Week celebrated his success in the very city where he'd first risen to prominence.

Elton chartered a plane to fly in his family, friends, Rocket Record Company employees, and a film crew to take in the spectacle. As UK music weekly *Sounds* wrote, Los Angeles was awash in Elton-mania, his songs constantly on the radio, every record shop boasting its own bounteous display of his merchandise, and his upcoming shows at Dodger Stadium the hottest ticket in town.

October 20 marked the US release date of *Rock of the Westies*. The first public event came on October 23, with the dedication of an Elton John star on Hollywood's Walk of Fame. Elton arrived at 6901 Hollywood Boulevard riding a golf cart adorned with oversized eyeglasses and a bowtie affixed to the front. He himself was no less ostentatious, attired in a green suit and bowler hat, both covered with stars bearing the names of other Walk of Famers. "I'm very, very honored, being British, to have my star on Hollywood Boulevard," he said to the screaming crowd, estimated at six thousand, large enough to stop traffic on the surrounding streets.

But, as he later revealed in his memoir, Elton felt awkward and uncomfortable at the event, masking his insecurity behind a joke: "I now declare this supermarket open!" But he couldn't keep unhappiness under wraps for long. The next day, in the middle of a party he was hosting at his rented home, he took an overdose of valium, announced to his guests what he'd done, then jumped into his swimming pool.

Elton played to 110,000 fans over two nights.

Hollywood Walk of Fame
ceremony, October 23, 1975.

The customized golf cart comes together at Barris Kustom City, October 19, 1975. Legendary car customizer George Barris is seated in the cart.

For Elton, it was a moment that symbolized the disconnect he felt in his life. Professionally, he was at a zenith, but personally, he felt depressed and alone. Though some accounts say his stomach was pumped, his memoir says he was given ipecac syrup which made him vomit, and he spent the night at home.

Despite the mishap, he went on to perform two of the most memorable shows of his career the same week. Dodger Stadium hadn't been used for a rock concert since The Beatles'

appearance there in 1966, when they'd played to a crowd of 45,000. Now Elton drew a total of 110,000 for two shows on October 25 and 26. He opened his set solo at the piano with "Your Song," the first in a mammoth three-and-a-half-hour show (including intermission) that was a well-paced mix of hits and deep album cuts.

The second half saw him wear one of his most iconic outfits: a sequined LA Dodgers uniform designed by Bob Mackie. During "Saturday Night's Alright for Fighting," he delighted the crowd by

climbing atop his piano with a baseball bat and hitting tennis balls into the audience. "Pinball Wizard" brought the show to a suitably rocking close.

Elton later said the shows were among those where everything comes together perfectly. He also recognized that Elton John Week marked a level of success that couldn't possibly be maintained, and he accepted that. Though he wasn't quite ready to confront his inner demons just yet.

31

· · · · · · · · · · · · · ·

THE FIRST UK SINGLES CHART TOPPER

· · · · · · · · · · · · · ·

"DON'T GO BREAKING MY HEART"

· · · · · · · · · · · · · ·

JUNE 21, 1976 (RELEASE)

Elton never hesitated to promote artists whose talents he admired. It's why he signed Kiki Dee to Rocket Records and why he invited her to join him in his first duet.

According to Elton's memoir, the song was written in 1975, when he was in Barbados with friends, including Dee and Bernie. He decided to write a duet for him and Dee to sing, first coming up with the jokey number "I'm Always on the Bonk." "Don't Go Breaking My Heart" was the more serious song, and, in contrast to the way they usually worked, Elton came up with the melody and the title first, then handed it off to Bernie to finish. Elton said Bernie never liked the song, which he considered "shallow pop." Perhaps that's why they used aliases for the songwriting credit; according to the label, the song was written by "Ann Orson and Carte Blanche."

Though Elton makes it sound like the song was always written with Kiki Dee in mind, other accounts say he'd originally intended to record it with Dusty Springfield. But Dee was a good fit for a song that was an homage of sorts to the duets Marvin Gaye and Tammi Terrell recorded for Motown. Elton recorded his vocal in Toronto, where he was working on the *Blue Moves* album (though the single would not

appear on the album). It was then sent to London, where Dee recorded her part.

But they were in the same room when they shot the song's video. It's a straight performance clip; the two are seen entering a recording studio, then they lip sync at the mic. Dee is a bit stiff in the opening moments, but Elton goes out of his way to make her feel at home, putting an arm around her and giving her smiles of encouragement. She did express some embarrassment about her outfit, a pair of loose, pink overalls. "If I'd known that it would have become such an iconic video, I might have been more concerned about what I was wearing," she told author Tom Doyle.

No matter. This bright and breezy slice of soul pop proved irresistible on both sides of the Atlantic, giving Elton his very first #1 single in the UK, his sixth in the US, and topping the charts in six other countries as well. Dee had previously been a backing vocalist for Elton when he performed live. Now she flew her parents to New York to see her perform her hit alongside Elton at his seven-night stand at Madison Square Garden in August.

Elton later recorded a new version for his album *Duets* with RuPaul; released as a single, the song reached #7 in the UK and #3 in *Billboard*'s Dance Club

Songs chart. Dee also appears on *Duets*, singing "True Love" with Elton, but she remains best known for "Don't Go Breaking My Heart" and retains a fondness for her singing partner. "I love working with him because as well as being hugely talented he's such a hoot," she told the *Express* in 2013. "He's a fascinating person, incredibly loyal and one of the funniest, most quick-witted people I've ever met."

Kiki Dee and Elton perform August 3, 1977.

The *Louder Than Concorde* tour, Pontic, Michigan, July 11, 1976.

"SOME PEOPLE DO GO BOTH WAYS"

COMING OUT IN ROLLING STONE

OCTOBER 7, 1976 (PUBLICATION)

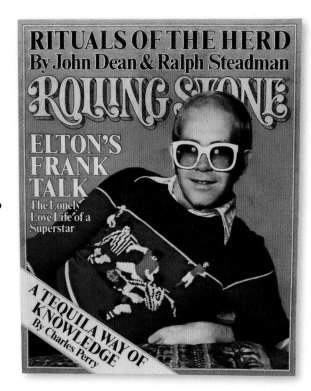

It wouldn't raise as many eyebrows today, but when Elton told *Rolling Stone* he was bisexual in 1976, public figures generally didn't admit to being anything other than heterosexual.

Elton met with reporter Cliff Jahr on August 18, the day after a weeklong run of shows at Madison Square Garden. He had previously brushed off questions about his sexuality, having told *Rolling Stone* in 1971, "I've got no time for love affairs." Jahr hoped to get Elton to open up a bit more.

So he was pleased that when he asked Elton if he could "get personal," Elton encouraged him to keep the tape recorder on. In response to the questions "What about Elton when he comes home at night? Does he have love and affection?" Elton replied that what he really wanted was love, speculating that a relationship with a woman might last longer than one with a man. This encouraged Jahr to go further: "You're bisexual?" Elton was indirect, but ultimately affirmative:

"There's nothing wrong with going to bed with someone of your same sex. I think everybody's bisexual to a certain degree. I don't think it's just me. It's not a bad thing to be."

Elton later said he felt he hadn't been "fudging the issue" by saying he was bisexual instead of gay, because he'd had a relationship with a woman before. Indeed, in 1968 he'd become engaged to Linda Woodrow, whom he'd met in Sheffield when Bluesology played there in 1967. His doubts about getting married led to a half-hearted suicide attempt at the home they shared— sticking his head in the oven but keeping the gas on low and leaving the window open. He finally found the nerve to break it off when he met up with Long John Baldry at a London club one night. "Wake up and smell the roses," his former bandmate bluntly told him, "You're gay." He wasn't sure about Baldry's character analysis but agreed his relationship with Woodrow should end. He and Bernie ended up moving back in with Elton's parents.

He was also somewhat untruthful when he told Jahr "I haven't met anybody I would like to settle down with." Until recently, Elton had been in just such a relationship with his manager, John Reid. The two met while John was working for EMI Records in London, and they'd become a couple at the time of Elton's first appearance in San Francisco in August 1970. They'd soon moved in together, but the romantic relationship ended in 1975 (Reid remained Elton's manager until 1998). Nor did he mention his sexual encounters were all with men. Elton's engagement to Woodrow might have made him able to claim he was "bisexual," but only just.

Elton's revelation provoked some fallout. It was deemed important enough to be covered by Walter Cronkite on the *CBS Evening News*, some US radio stations stopped playing his records, and Elton's future songwriting partner Gary Osborne said sales slumped in middle America (Elton contended sales had been steadily dropping from the heights of *Goodbye Yellow Brick Road* anyway). Elton himself didn't think it was that big of an issue, though he joked to Jahr, "It's going to be terrible with my football club."

Hilversum, Netherlands, 1976.

PART 3

CHANGE IT UP TO SHAKE IT UP, 1977–1989

33

"I WASN'T DOING ANYTHING THAT NIGHT"

THE SHOREDITCH COLLEGE SHOW

JUNE 17, 1977

Of all the places you'd least expect to find Elton John performing, a small college in suburban London would likely be among them. Yet that's where Elton ended up giving one of his most unexpected performances, simply because his housekeeper answered the doorbell.

In 1976, Elton told his band he wanted to take time off from the road. For the next two years, his appearances were limited to one-off engagements and charity events. As a result, he ended up spending more time at home. Which is where he was on June 17, watching a tennis match on television when his housekeeper informed him that students from Shoreditch College had stopped by. Soul singer Jimmy Helms had been scheduled to appear at their Valedictory Ball that evening, but he'd unexpectedly canceled. The students knew that Elton lived not far away and as a lark decided to drop by and see if he might consider filling in.

To their amazement, Elton impulsively agreed, on condition they provide a

grand piano for him to play. When school officials wouldn't let the students move either of the chapel's grand pianos into the main hall, they simply decided to have Elton perform in the chapel. Word spread among the student body, though many thought it had to be a joke. It was hard to believe that a star of the magnitude of Elton John would deign to appear at Shoreditch.

But sure enough, at 9:30 p.m., Elton arrived. After a brief soundcheck, he played a six-song set: "Crocodile Rock," "Daniel," "Rocket Man," "Your Song," "I Heard It Through the Grapevine," and "Bennie and the Jets." By the time he'd finished, the chapel was stuffed to capacity with disbelieving students.

Elton further thrilled his audience by staying on for a few hours afterward, chatting and telling stories. As payment, he was offered a bottle of whiskey, which he turned down, saying he had plenty at home. But he did accept a commemorative pint glass. A fine souvenir from a most unexpected night out.

34

"IT'S TIME TO LIGHT THE LIGHTS!"

A very special duet of "Don't Go Breaking My Heart."

THE MUPPET SHOW

JANUARY 8, 1978 (US BROADCAST)

Elton was a natural to appear on *The Muppet Show*, surrounded by characters as colorful and outrageous as he was.

Jim Henson's Muppets had gained great exposure as part of the cast of the children's educational program *Sesame Street*. *The Muppet Show* was designed to appeal to an older demographic. While no US networks were interested in the proposed program, Lew Grade agreed to co-produce the show for his UK company Associated Television (ATV), and the episodes were filmed at ATV's studios in Elstree, England. *The Muppet Show* debuted on September 5, 1976; the last episode was broadcast on March 15, 1981.

ATV licensed the show to countries around the world, and it quickly became a success due to its quirky humor and the range of guest stars who gamely agreed to be the only human on the set. You might see Broadway star Ethel

Merman giving Miss Piggy some singing pointers; *Monty Python* alum John Cleese appearing in the show's sci-fi parody, *Pigs in Space*; or Rudolf Nureyev dancing in a ballet piece called "Swine Lake."

Always up for having some fun in performance, Elton was an obvious choice. Even the visual settings were obvious. Where else would Elton (looking like some kind of exotic bird, with multicolored feathers sprouting from his shoulders) play "Crocodile Rock" but in a swamp with crocodiles emerging from the watery depths to sing along with him on the chorus?

After the cast fails to impress the show's host, Kermit the Frog, with a riotous, unrecognizable version of "Bennie and the Jets," Elton (in a purple jacket with flared shoulders) takes over and shows them how it's done. "Goodbye Yellow Brick Road" gets the most formal presentation, with Elton, sporting a yellow jacket with sparkly trim and a black bowler hat, seated at the piano throughout, backed by the show's in-house rock band, Dr. Teeth and the Electric Mayhem.

For the grand finale, Elton changes to a pink bejeweled jumpsuit that would've done Elvis proud, and gleefully introduces "a wonderful lady I've always wanted to work with and sing with"—Miss Piggy. "Oh Elton, have you been waiting long, poopsie?" the show's resident diva, clad in silver, coos as she comes on stage. "It seems like an eternity!" Elton replies, as the two go into "Don't Go Breaking My Heart." The pair cuddles throughout, Miss Piggy getting so worked up she kisses Elton's bare chest, later shouting, "Eat your heart out, Kiki!"

Coming during a year when Elton gave no full-scale concerts, his *The Muppet Show* appearance was a welcome treat for his fans, who were eager for any news about him.

Elton's *The Muppet Show* appearance was a welcome treat for his fans.

35

THE NEW WORDSMITH

A SINGLE MAN

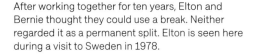

After working together for ten years, Elton and Bernie thought they could use a break. Neither regarded it as a permanent split. Elton is seen here during a visit to Sweden in 1978.

OCTOBER 1978 (US RELEASE)

OCTOBER 10, 1978 (UK RELEASE)

When *A Single Man* was released, people debated the title's meaning. Did it refer to Elton's relationship status? Or was it a reference to the fact that this was the first album he'd released that had no contributions from his songwriting partner, Bernie Taupin? Either—or both—could be true. One thing was certain: It was an album that saw Elton making a fresh start.

After working together for ten years, Elton and Bernie thought they could use a break from each other. Neither

regarded it as a permanent split; they simply felt they could benefit from some time apart. Elton already had a lyricist in mind, Gary Osborne, who'd written the English lyrics for Kiki Dee's first hit, "Amoureuse," as well as lyrics for the concept album *Jeff Wayne's War of the Worlds* (1978).

The album also marked the first time Elton's name appeared as a co-producer, sharing the job not with his longtime producer Gus Dudgeon, but another new person, Clive Franks, who'd previously served as an engineer on Elton's albums. Elton also relied primarily on session musicians, including Franks, who played bass.

Osborne's writing style was more direct and straightforward, in contrast to Taupin's more literary leanings. Elton also contributed more lyrical themes and ideas to the songs. Most of the songs address love in its many permutations. The celebratory "I Don't Care" sees the joy of love as helping to overcome all obstacles. "Shine on Through" is a soaring ballad that looks at the end of a love affair; "Shooting Star" covers the same terrain in a more restrained fashion. "It Ain't Going to Be Easy" is a searing look at infidelity, with a stinging guitar line echoing its

accusatory tone throughout. Then there's the cheeky "Big Dipper," a tale of cruising and pickups with plenty of innuendo ("Did you learn a few new licks?") and backing vocals from members of Watford Football Club.

"Georgia" is the kind of song Bernie might've written, a gospel-drenched ode to the southern state where Elton would have a home one day. The oddest track—indeed, one of the strangest songs Elton's ever recorded—would have to be "Madness," about a terrorist's swath of destruction, set to a new wave–ish beat.

Overall, the album was rather patchy. While some songs were stronger than others, there were no clear standouts.

Not surprisingly, the album received mixed reviews, though it fared better in the UK (peaking at #8) than the US (peaking at #15). The first two singles also did better in the UK. "Part-Time Love," an upbeat song about the commitment-shy, reached #15 UK versus #22 US. The largely instrumental "Song for Guy," a melancholy piece that Elton named after Guy Burchett, a young employee at Rocket Records who'd been killed in a motorcycle accident, reached #4 in the UK and did well in other countries but didn't even reach the Top 100 in the US. "Return to Paradise," a dreamy song about parted lovers, failed to chart on either side of the Atlantic.

36

FINDING PHILLY SOUL

......

"MAMA CAN'T BUY YOU LOVE"

......

JUNE 1979 (RELEASE)

Prior to recording *A Single Man*, Elton had been working in the studio with producer Thom Bell. One of the resulting songs became a hit a year after *Single Man*'s release; another wouldn't crack the charts until twenty-six years after the original sessions.

Elton had decided he wanted to take a backseat in his next recording venture, working primarily as a vocalist, not even playing piano. He reached out to Bell, a producer and songwriter who was one of the stars of the "Philly Soul" scene of the 1970s, having produced hits for the O'Jays, the Stylistics, and the Spinners, as well as numerous acts from the Philadelphia International Records stable. Elton was a huge fan of Bell's work ("I just loved the way his records sounded," he told *The Weekly of Metropolitan Seattle*), and was excited at the prospect of working with him.

So in October 1977, he flew to Seattle, where Bell was then living, recording at Kaye-Smith Studio. During the four-day session, Elton picked up some useful tips from his producer on proper breathing techniques and singing in a lower register.

Elton ended up recording six songs; Bell added further overdubbing at Sigma Sound Studios in Philadelphia. But Elton wasn't entirely satisfied with how the tracks came out. Though he praised the "luxurious strings" Bell had added, he ultimately felt they were "too saccharine," so he cancelled the recording sessions that had been set up for November and the project was put aside.

Two years later, having overcome his hesitation, Elton decided to have three tracks remixed by Clive Franks, and "Mama Can't Buy You Love," "Are You Ready for Love," and "Three Way Love

Affair" were released on an EP in October 1979. It was a different sound for Elton, and to a longtime fan his voice might well have sounded muted, without the taut, reedy quality evident in tracks like "Crocodile Rock" or "Bennie and the Jets." But the musicians (Philadelphia's famed studio musicians who used the moniker MFSB, for "Mother Father Sister Brother") and backing vocalists (none other than the Spinners) gave them just the right feeling for the dance floor. "Mama Can't Buy You Love" reached #9 in the US.

Twenty years on, *The Complete Thom Bell Sessions* was released, featuring all the songs from the session: the three songs from the 1979 EP (using the original Thom Bell mixes, not the Clive Franks remixes) and three previously unreleased tracks, "Country Love Song," "Nice and Slow," and "Shine on Through." "Nice and Slow" was co-written with Bernie, while "Shine on Through" was one of the first tracks Elton wrote with Gary Osborne (it had been re-recorded for *A Single Man*).

And that still wasn't the end of the story. Ashley Beedle remixed "Are You Ready for Love" and released it on a 12-inch single in August 2003; the song reached #1 on the UK singles chart, and #1 on *Billboard*'s Dance Club chart.

Elton had cited his song "Philadelphia Freedom" as his attempt to capture the Philly Soul sound himself. And working with one of the main architects of that sound, that's exactly what he was able to do.

Back in the USA tour, Hill Auditorium, Ann Arbor, Michigan, October 2, 1979.

37

FROM RUSSIA WITH LOVE

THE RUSSIAN TOUR

Getting a leg up, May 21 to 24 at the Oktyabrsky Grand Concert Hall, Leningrad—the first of the USSR dates.

MAY 21–28, 1979

In May 1979, Elton John became the first major western rock act to play behind the Iron Curtain, taking his music to the heart of the Union of Soviet Socialist Republics (USSR).

Following the release of *A Single Man*, Elton decided to launch his first full-scale tour in three years. He stuck to the same two-person setup he'd been using recently, playing solo for the first half of the show (on either a Steinway grand piano or electric Yamaha CP80), then bringing on percussionist Ray Cooper to join him.

"The show was not an extravaganza," Cooper explained. "It was about the music, and the drama of Bernie Taupin's lyrics and Elton's wonderful melodies. It was a theatrical show. What I was there for, I think, was to add color to the drama."

Elton was interested in playing places he'd never been to before, and put forth the idea that he might play Russia to his promoter, Harvey Goldsmith. Goldsmith sent the request to the British Foreign Office, who passed it on to the Russian Ministry of Culture. A Russian promoter was then dispatched to see Elton's show in Oxford, England, on April 17, to judge its suitability for Russian audiences. The only western pop acts who'd previously performed in the USSR were vocal group Boney M. and the mild-mannered Cliff Richard.

Duly approved, Elton, Cooper, and an entourage including journalists, Elton's mother and stepfather, and the inevitable film crew, arrived in Russia the following month. Eight performances were scheduled from May 21 to 24 at the Oktyabrsky Grand Concert Hall, Leningrad (now St. Petersburg), and May 25 to 28 at the Rossiya Concert Hall in Moscow.

The two musicians were puzzled at first by the audience's restrained response. Then they learned that older Soviet officials were given the prime seats down front, while the younger, more enthusiastic fans were kept at the back. But Cooper's exuberant antics—he, after all, could run around the stage while Elton was stuck behind the piano—always managed to get at least some of the crowd on their feet by the show's end.

The crowd had gone wild when Elton kicked his piano stool away on the first night; officials sternly told him not to excite the audience in this fashion again. Despite official admonitions to the contrary, he always snuck in a bit of the Beatles' "Back in the USSR" during a medley.

The final night of the tour was broadcast by the BBC and footage from the tour appeared in the 1979 documentary *To Russia . . . With Elton*. In 2019, an edited version of the complete concert was released on the album *Live From Moscow 1979* for Record Store Day; the following year, the show was reissued for the general public on vinyl and CD.

The shows left an indelible impression on those lucky enough to see them, and

Cooper said numerous people over the years have told him how much the shows meant: "When you come across people that say you've changed their lives through music, then, yeah, you know you've done your job. And what a beautiful job to do."

Moscow's Rossiya Hotel, May 29, 1979.

With mother Sheila Farebrother and stepfather Fred Farebrother in the Kremlin, Moscow, May 27, 1979.

FOUR HUNDRED THOUSAND ELTON FANS CAN'T BE WRONG

THE CENTRAL PARK CONCERT

SEPTEMBER 13, 1980

Elton began the 1970s with a breakthrough show at the LA Troubadour playing to an audience of five hundred people. He ushered in the new decade by playing to a crowd eight hundred times that number.

The American/Canadian leg of his 1980 tour took in forty-eight shows in forty-one different cities, and his return to the Big Apple was set to be a spectacular event. Held at the Great Lawn in Central Park, the show was free, with proceeds from merchandise going to the city's Department of Parks and Recreation.

It was a perfect fall day and the crowd eventually swelled to an estimated half a million people—the largest audience Elton had ever performed to up to that time. After opening with "Funeral for a Friend"/"Love Lies Bleeding" (the first of five songs from *Goodbye Yellow Brick Road*), the set encompassed three songs from his latest album (1980's *21 at 33*), much-loved signature songs ("Rocket Man," "Philadelphia Freedom"), and recent hits ("Ego"). The second set opened with a riveting "Saturday Night's Alright for Fighting," Elton waiting for just the right moment to kick away the piano stool—a repeated bit of business that never failed to fire up the audience.

After a manic "Bennie and the Jets" (which ran ten minutes), Elton dedicated his next song to a friend who "only lives just over the road." It turned out to be John Lennon's "Imagine" (John wasn't at the show to hear it, but he and his wife Yoko turned up at the afterparty). And an unexpected "guest" made an appearance during the main set's closing number, "Someone Saved My Life Tonight:" a female fan who made it onstage to kiss Elton on the cheek and was allowed to sit next to him while he finished the song.

There was no doubt of an encore, but a puzzling delay had everybody wondering what was going on. Unbeknownst to the audience, Elton was backstage struggling to get into his surprise costume: Donald Duck. He'd thought it would be a great joke to come onstage as the crabby Disney cartoon character. But he hadn't anticipated how difficult the Bob Mackie–designed outfit would be to put on, struggling to fit his arms and legs into the wrong holes, becoming helpless with laughter over his predicament.

When he finally waddled on stage to cheers and guffaws, there were new problems to contend with. The flipper-sized feet made it difficult to walk. And the duck's bottom was so large he couldn't sit down properly, forcing him to stand while playing the final numbers. Though he continued laughing during "Your Song"—every time he caught one of his bandmate's incredulous expressions he'd break out in a "fit of the giggles"—he persevered and closed out the show with high-energy versions of "Bite Your Lip (Get Up and Dance!)" and the Little Richard cover "Good Golly, Miss Molly."

Elton called it "A fantastic show," which ended up raising $75,000 for the parks department. And it demonstrated he was quite comfortable commanding the attention of an enormous audience. There would be more to come.

Performing for
400,000 fans in
Central Park,
New York City.

39

"LOOKING LIKE A TRUE SURVIVOR"

TOO LOW FOR ZERO

MAY 23, 1983 (US RELEASE)

JUNE 1983 (UK RELEASE)

AIR Recording Studios in Montserrat, 1982.

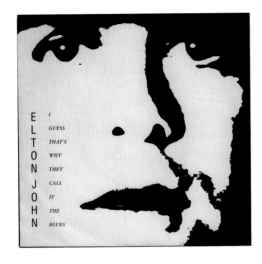

Too Low for Zero was the first album since 1976's *Blue Moves* to be almost entirely written by the John/Taupin team, putting Elton back in the UK Top 10, and giving him the biggest album sales since *Rock of the Westies*.

After *A Single Man* and *Victim of Love*, Elton's next three albums each featured a few songs by Bernie. But he and Elton realized it would be more beneficial to work on an entire album together, "to make the partnership really click," as Elton put it. For his part, Bernie told journalist Paul Grein, "I think it was at that time that we both realized how much we wanted this." The album would also see them working with the original Elton John Band—guitarist Davey Johnstone, bassist Dee Murray, and drummer Nigel Olsson—for the first time since the *Captain Fantastic* album.

Elton felt like he was back working with a "well-oiled machine" and that the songs had a new freshness. That's certainly true of the two songs the album is best known for, "I Guess That's Why They Call It the Blues" and "I'm Still Standing," both fan favorites which became staples in Elton's setlists. The former song, which reached #4 US and #5 UK, is a yearning number about the

"blues" that come when you're separated from your romantic partner; the harmonica solo is by Stevie Wonder. This is the one song on the album that had another writer: Davey Johnstone received a co-writing credit for the music. "I'm Still Standing" is the flipside to such a situation, a spirited kiss-off to a former love that became something of a theme song for Elton, seemingly referencing his own ability to triumph over adversity; it reached #12 in the US, #4 in the UK.

There was also a different sound on the album, with synthesizers being more prominent. Elton had wanted to get away from having such a heavily piano-based sound and ended up writing most of the album's songs on a synthesizer for the first time. It gave the album a modern feel perfectly in keeping with the synth-pop style of the early 80s. It also had the result of brightening the mood of ostensibly downbeat songs, such as the title track, with its toe-tapping beat belying the song's theme of depression. And "Kiss the Bride," the album's third single (#25 US, #20 UK), ushers in its story of a man watching his former girlfriend getting married to someone else with a thick bed of chords pounded out on a Yamaha synth.

Though the lower chart placing of "Kiss the Bride" indicated waning public interest, a fourth single was nonetheless released, "Cold as Christmas (In the Middle of the Year)," a lovelorn song about trying—and failing—to spark life back into a relationship on a tropical holiday. But the single (which featured Kiki Dee on backing vocals) didn't spark much life on the charts; it reached #33 in the UK and wasn't released in the US.

But overall, *Too Low for Zero* revived Elton's career and showed he was going to be a commercial force in the 1980s.

40

LOVE AND MARRIAGE, PART ONE

ELTON WEDS RENATE BLAUEL

FEBRUARY 14, 1984

Elton and Renate after their wedding ceremony in Sydney, February 14, 1984.

The newlyweds' luggage arrives at London's Heathrow Airport, March 1984.

Despite his claim of being bisexual, Elton's friends were shocked when he announced that he was marrying a woman. But to Elton, it made a kind of sense. His relationships with men hadn't worked out; maybe he'd fare better with a woman.

Elton met Renate Blauel, a German living in London, when she served as a tape operator during the recording of *Too Low for Zero*. On his next album, *Breaking Hearts*, she'd been promoted to engineer. The album was partially recorded at AIR Recording Studios in Montserrat, and it was here that their friendship blossomed. Elton found himself spending more and more time with Renate, drawn by her intelligence and sense of humor.

She brushed off his first proposal of marriage. But Elton was persistent; he felt marriage to her would "solve all my problems at a stroke." When everyone had relocated to Sydney in preparation for his next tour, which was set to begin in New Zealand, Elton proposed to Renate again, while they were dining at an Indian restaurant. This time she said yes.

When the couple returned to their hotel and announced their engagement to their friends, everyone at first thought it was a joke. When they realized Elton was serious, there was a rush to arrange the wedding, which would be held in just four days' time. Given the distance and timing, neither Elton's nor Renate's parents attended. Bernie and Elton's manager John Reid were the best men. Following the ceremony there was a lavish £50,000 reception at the Sebel Town House hotel.

Renate called Elton "the nicest guy I've ever met. I've heard all sorts of stories about Elton and that he's supposed to be bisexual, but that doesn't worry me." But problems in the marriage soon arose. Sometime in 1986, the couple separated and reconciled. It was noted that they seemed to spend more and more time apart. Newspapers were quick to report that when Elton underwent surgery for cysts on his vocal cords in 1986, his wife was not with him.

After it was reported that Renate hadn't attended Elton's fortieth birthday party, an official statement was released on

March 27, 1987, confirming that the couple were separating. But when he appeared on the UK talk show *One-to-One* the following month, Elton still held out hope that it wasn't a permanent break: "The marriage isn't over, per se. We just separated for a little while. That happens to every marriage."

And the two did reconcile for a time. But it was not to last. The following year, on November 18, 1988, it was announced that the two planned to divorce "by mutual consent." Because of an agreement to not discuss intimate details about their lives, the circumstances of their marriage and the specifics of the divorce settlement have never been made public.

Elton later admitted that he'd married to avoid facing up to his real problem— substance abuse. "I thought: now I'll become happy. But the problem was I still stuck cocaine up my nose and drank a bottle of Scotch a day." He also told the *Sydney Morning Herald*, "I loved Renate. . . . It is one of the things I regret most in my life, hurting her."

41

"MY YEARS AT THE CLUB WERE SO MAGNIFICENT"

ELTON'S TEAM MAKES THE FA CUP FINAL

MAY 19, 1984

After years of hard work, it was a dream come true for Elton and all fans of Watford Football Club. For the first time in the team's history, they made it all the way through the Football Association Challenge Cup to the main event: the FA Cup Final.

Elton had been a loyal supporter of Watford FC since he went to his first match at the age of six. He loved everything about attending the matches: riding the train to Watford, the walk through the town to the stadium grounds at Vicarage Road, claiming his favorite spot on the terraces. His penchant for statistics meant that he kept track of sports scores the way he noted chart placings. It was also a family interest—two of his cousins, Roy Dwight and John Ashen, played for Fulham FC.

In 1974, when Elton learned Watford was having financial difficulties, he found the time in his busy schedule to play a benefit concert at Vicarage Road on May 5. He became vice president of the club, and in 1976 purchased the organization, becoming president and chairman. By then, the club had dropped to the bottom of the Fourth Division. In an effort to turn the club's fortunes around, he hired a new manager, Graham Taylor, in part because Taylor had brought his previous team, Lincoln City, out of the Fourth Division.

Elton's strategy paid off. At the end of Taylor's first season, Watford won the Fourth Division title and continued progressing upward. But for Elton, his ownership was about more than winning games. His work with the club took him out of the sycophantic realm of entertainment. None of the people he dealt with in the football world treated

Clowning at Watford FC's Vicarage Road stadium, April 1974. Elton has been a loyal supporter since he went to his first match at the age of six.

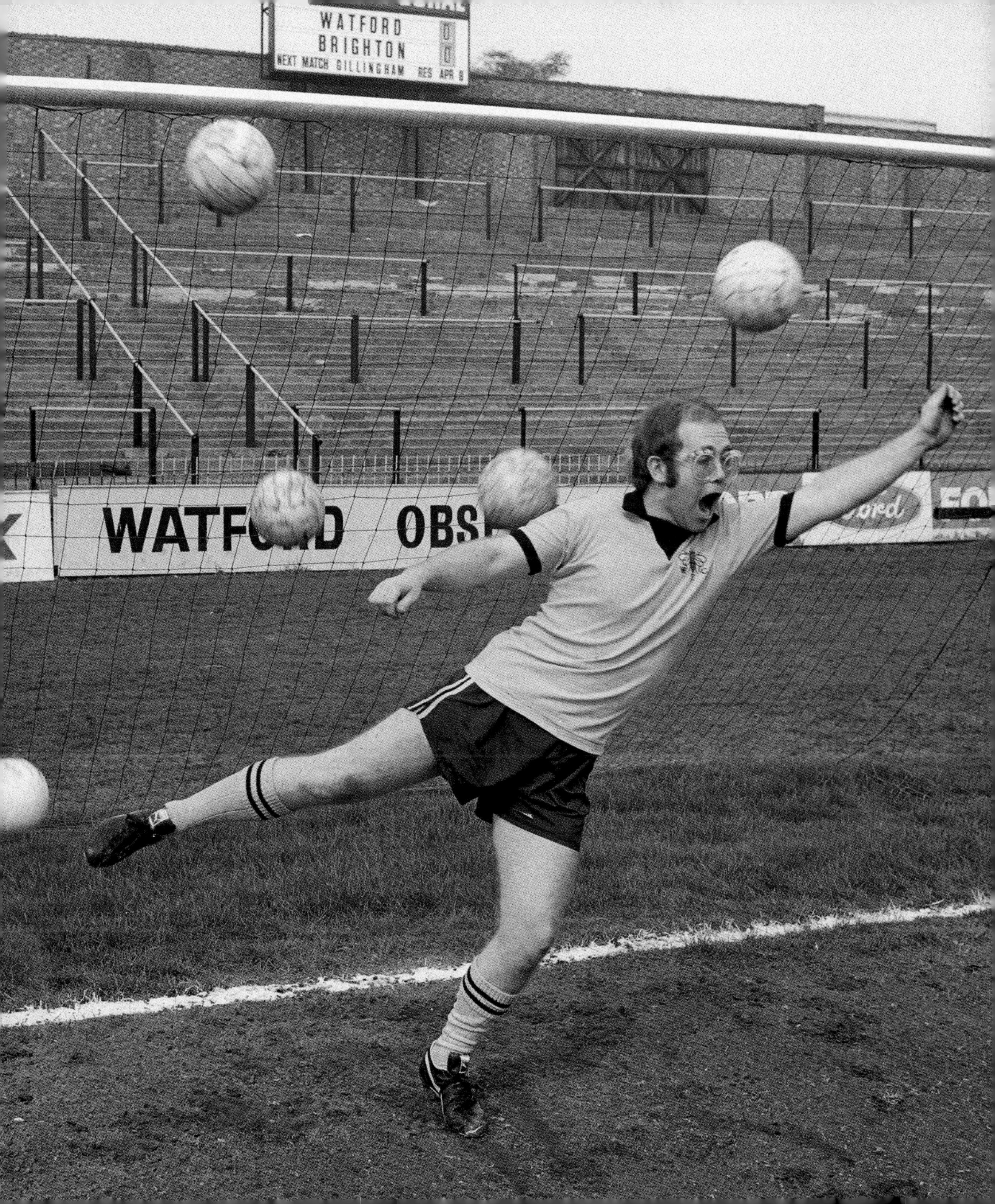
WATFORD 0
BRIGHTON 0
NEXT MATCH GILLINGHAM RES APR 8

On the pitch before
a match, May 1984.

him with special deference because he was Elton John. Indeed, Taylor once berated him for showing up at a game hungover, saying he was letting the club down. It was a lecture Elton admitted he deserved. And he relished the sense of community: "When I didn't feel I had any love in my personal life, I knew I had love from the club and the supporters."

With Taylor's help, and Elton's funding, the club was able to hire new players and build new stands. In the 1981–82 season, Watford advanced to the First Division for the first time in its history. Though Watford lost the FA Cup Final to Everton 2–0, it was a proud achievement for a club that had been at the bottom of the barrel a few years before.

Elton's involvement with Watford continued over the years: selling the club in 1990, buying it again in 1997 (and selling it again later), serving as Honorary Life President, playing benefits to raise money for the organization. In December 2014, the renovated East Stand on the Vicarage Road grounds was named after Elton, with lyrics from "Your Song" painted on the back. It was a fitting honor for a man who said, on the day the new stand was opened, "I love football, and I always will, and Watford is embedded in my heart."

42

"THE ROCK WORLD CAME TOGETHER"

LIVE AID

JULY 13, 1985

Elton performed a six-song set at Live Aid's London venue, Wembley Stadium.

Live Aid was the largest rock charity event of its time, with a dazzling array of the world's top musicians coming together to raise funds for African famine relief. And Elton was one of the first to sign on.

The roots of Live Aid date back to October 1984, when Boomtown Rats lead singer Bob Geldof watched a BBC news report about widespread famine in Ethiopia. He approached his friend Midge Ure of Ultravox, and the two wrote the song "Do They Know It's Christmas?" Geldof then tapped numerous musician friends (Sting, Phil Collins, members of U2 and Duran Duran, among others) to record the song as a charity single; the all-star collective was named "Band Aid."

The single went on sale in the UK in November and topped the charts; in the US, it was released in December and reached #13. The single would eventually raise millions for the cause. Geldof's next step was to stage a benefit concert on a scale nobody had previously dreamed of: two concerts, held the same day at Wembley Stadium in London and JFK Stadium in Philadelphia, broadcast live around the world.

Geldof mentioned the concert to Elton in March 1985 when the two met at that year's Ivor Novello Awards ceremony, where Geldof won a prize for "Do They Know It's Christmas?" Elton agreed to be involved and was rewarded with one of the show's longer sets. He took the

stage in a rather sedate outfit: black trousers and a black Nehru-style jacket decorated with gold, silver, red, and green. A black fez with a purple feather completed the ensemble.

After being introduced by comedian Billy Connolly as coming direct from "Planet Windsor" (Windsor being the town of Elton's primary residence), Elton got the crowd going with "I'm Still Standing," which led into an equally crowd-pleasing "Bennie and the Jets." After slowing down the pace with "Rocket Man," he brought Kiki Dee, serving as one of the backing singers, down center stage for "Don't Go Breaking My Heart." He then welcomed Wham! To the stage, with George Michael turning in a powerful lead vocal

performance of "Don't Let the Sun Go Down on Me." The set closed with an unusual choice: a cover of Marvin Gaye's "Can I Get a Witness."

Backstage, Elton hosted a barbecue, inviting the day's other artists to come by. When Queen's Freddie Mercury dropped in, he made the cheeky observation, "Darling! What the fuck were you wearing on your head? You looked like the Queen Mother!"

Elton's set has never been released in its entirety, but four of the six songs appear on the four-DVD *Live Aid* box set.

With Live Aid organizer Bob Geldof in June 1985.

43

ELTON'S TOP EIGHT

On the set of the "Heartache All Over the World" video shoot, Oakland, California, August 14, 1986.

DESERT ISLAND DISCS

JUNE 1, 1986 (UK BROADCAST)

As a lifelong record fan, Elton was unsurprisingly an avid *Desert Island Discs* listener, eager to share his own selections when he was invited to appear on the famed program.

The long-running British radio show has invited guests to choose the eight recordings they'd take with them if they were marooned on a desert island, along with one book and a luxury item. Actor Vic Oliver was the designated "castaway" on the first show, broadcast on the BBC Forces Programme on January 29, 1942 (at the time of this writing, the show was being broadcast on BBC Radio 4).

Michael Parkinson was the host for Elton's appearance. Elton's musical selections were quite diverse and brought up some interesting memories. One song that left a strong impression on him was Pink Floyd's "Shine On You

Crazy Diamond." He recalled vacationing in Barbados in 1976 and meeting a teenage boy dealing with cancer, holding hands with him as they watched the sunset while the Floyd song played in the background. Three years later, he was happy to encounter the young man again after a concert in Washington, DC, his cancer now in remission.

Given his love of soul music, Nina Simone's performance of "I Put a Spell on You" was an obvious choice. But "Nimrod," from Edward Elgar's *The Enigma Variations* (as performed by the London Symphony Orchestra) was perhaps more unexpected. Elton explained that this piece was a favorite and he always made sure he had a cassette recording of it when traveling.

He then opted for something more upbeat: the Rolling Stones' "Let It Rock," a track to "go crazy" too. William Hendry

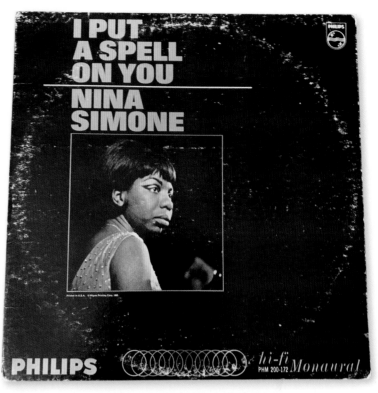

A few of Elton's favorite things, as mentioned on
BBC's *Desert Island Discs* program, June 1986.

More scenes from the "Heartache All Over the World" video shoot, Oakland, California, August 14, 1986.

Monk's hymn "Abide with Me" was a natural choice as "the anthem of soccer," in Parkinson's words, leading into a conversation about Elton's involvement with Watford FC. He calls Thelonious Monk's "Misterioso" "an extraordinary piece of music," choosing a performance of the number by Carla Bley, pointing out that Kenny Kirkland's solo was "one of the most beautiful piano solos I've ever heard."

Interestingly, he chose John Lennon's cover of "Stand By Me" instead of one of Lennon's own compositions. "They're all such personal songs, and the lyrics are very, very personal," he explained, perhaps a reflection of how painful Lennon's loss still was to him. And he found the good spirits of "Wake Me Up Before You Go-Go" by Wham! infectious. "I just happen to love this record because it sounds like an old Motown record," he said, adding, "George Michael will be around for a long time."

His book choice was *Interview with a Vampire* by Anne Rice, "which lets your imagination run riot." Luxury item? That would be a telephone, so he could keep up on all the gossip, as well as keeping track of Watford's matches.

In between song choices, Elton chatted with Parkinson about his career. Among the interesting tidbits shared was how he admired Lennon's kindness and his ability to connect with anyone he met, regardless of their background. In retrospect, one comment in particular stands out: Elton's ambition to write a musical one day. The opportunity would come before too long.

44

A CLASSICAL MASHUP

With the "fright wig" at Sydney Entertainment Centre, December 1, 1986—the first night of a thirteen-date stand.

LIVE IN AUSTRALIA

DECEMBER 14, 1986 (RECORDING)

Elton had played with classical musicians before. But he'd never done an entire live set with an orchestra, let alone toured with one. So his plans to do so during the Australian leg of his 1986 world tour were ambitious. But there would be some unexpected bumps along the way.

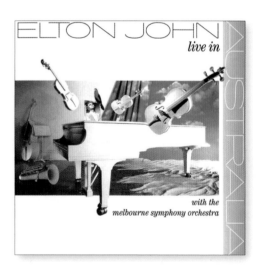

The main issue was Elton's voice, which began giving him problems toward the end of the US leg of his tour. By the time he played Madison Square Garden in September, he found he could sing while onstage, but that he'd lost his speaking voice when offstage. He tried his usual remedies of hot drinks and not speaking, but the problem persisted.

By the time Elton arrived Down Under for the Australian leg, set to begin on November 5 in Brisbane, he was especially concerned. His singing voice was now affected as well, to the point that he could no longer control it. It didn't bode well for the scheduled performances with the Melbourne Symphony Orchestra, especially because the final date in Sydney was going to be broadcast live and recorded for future release.

When the tour reached Sydney, Elton finally saw a doctor and learned that he had cysts on his vocal cords. If they turned out to be cancerous, he was at risk of having his larynx removed, meaning he'd never speak or sing again. It was alarming news and Elton's doctor advised him to cancel the rest of the tour and have surgery as soon as possible.

Though Elton was frightened by the diagnosis, he was determined to see the tour through to the end. It wasn't simply a matter of the financial losses he'd incur if the remaining dates were canceled. If he was going to lose his voice, he wanted to keep singing as long as possible.

So the show went on at Sydney's Entertainment Centre. For the show's first half, when he played with his band, he wore a black suit covered with stars, topped by a pink "fright wig" and new wave-style sunglasses. For the second half, as a nod to the classical musicians, he dressed in a white suit with tails and matching wig, "like Mozart had joined a glam rock band." But the most extraordinary element was his voice. Though noticeably rougher, it gives a gravitas to his performance. He's also able to sing with great forcefulness; "Don't Let the Sun Go Down on Me" is particularly masterful.

The following month, on January 3, Elton underwent surgery in Sydney. Happily, the cysts turned out to be benign. The quality of his voice did change, but he felt it was for the better, finding that his deeper timbre gave him more resonance.

He played only one date in 1987, an AIDS benefit at Wembley Stadium in April, allowing his throat to fully heal.

Fans could content themselves with *Live in Australia with the Melbourne Symphony Orchestra*, released in June 1987, featuring most, but not all, of the orchestral set. Portions of the entire show were later released on VHS, LaserDisc, and DVD.

"Like Mozart had joined a glam rock band." With the Melbourne Symphony Orchestra, November 11, 1986.

45

. . . .

GOING TO THE HIGHEST BIDDER

. . . .

ELTON'S GRAND AUCTION

. . . .

SEPTEMBER 6–9, 1988

When most people hold a garage sale, they might end up making a few hundred dollars. When Elton decided to clear out the clutter in his home, he came away with $8.2 million.

The clearing out began when Elton realized that he could no longer play on his own squash court because it was filled with packing crates containing items that he'd purchased. And there was no point in unpacking them because there was no room in his house—or any building on his property—to put their contents ("It's like walking into a warehouse" he said of his over-stuffed home). So he decided he'd simply get rid of everything. Perhaps not coincidentally, his marriage to Renate Blauel had ended; maybe the time seemed right to make a sweeping change.

It took three days to pack up all of Elton's possessions. He did hang on to some items: his bed, his cars, original radio scripts from the British comedy radio series *The Goon Show*, and four paintings (two Magrittes, one by Francis Bacon, and one by Patrick Proctor). And, of course, his record collection. He then moved to London, where he lived for two years while his Windsor home was remodeled.

Such was the bounty, the items to be auctioned were not only displayed in advance at London's Victoria and Albert Museum, they were also sent on the road and exhibited in New York, Los Angeles, Sydney, and Tokyo. The exhibits offered a fascinating glimpse not only at Elton's professional life (costumes, tour memorabilia, record awards), but also his personal life (Tiffany lamps, Bugatti furniture, Cartier watches, Elvis Presley's autograph). If you couldn't make it to the exhibits or the auction itself, you could always purchase the catalog (which ran to four volumes). A pile of his possessions was

also displayed on the cover of his 1988 album *Reg Strikes Back*.

Elton's belongings were divided into four categories and auctioned accordingly at Sotheby's London: costumes and memorabilia on September 6, jewelry on September 7, art nouveau and art deco on September 8, and "Diverse Collections" on September 9. The auction was expected to bring in $5 million, but bids vastly exceeded the original estimates. A painting by Magritte sold for $119,700. The Hard Rock Cafe bought a pair of sunglasses with lights that spelled out E-L-T-O-N for nearly $17,000. The "Pinball Wizard" Doc Martens boots he'd worn in *Tommy* were purchased by R. Griggs Group Ltd (appropriately, the manufacturer of Doc Martens) for $20,200. Even the banners that hung outside of Sotheby's advertising the auction were sold.

Elton found that ridding himself of his possessions was a kind of purging. But it didn't mean that he was planning to adopt a minimalist lifestyle. He was simply "changing direction," as he told United Press International. "I'm doing this so we can start again." Indeed, in 2003, he enlisted Sotheby's to auction off the contents of his London home, bringing in $2.3 million. Shopping was one addiction Elton never got over.

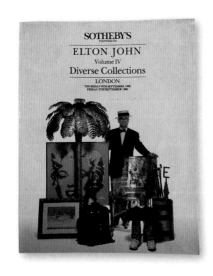

Promotional photo taken for the 1988 Sotheby's affair.

46

"YOU CAN'T TELL LIES ABOUT ME"

THE SUN LAWSUIT

DECEMBER 12, 1988
(SETTLEMENT)

It was a moment of vindication. From the time the British tabloid *The Sun* had begun printing scurrilous stories about him, Elton had been advised not to sue. But he wasn't about to back down in the face of such obvious lies. He took the tabloid to court—and won.

The saga began on February 25, 1987, when the paper published a story headlined ELTON IN VICE BOYS SCANDAL. The source, a young man referred to as "Graham X," claimed Elton had used him to procure "rent boys" (young male prostitutes) for a party at the home of Rod Stewart's manager. More stories followed over the next week, alleging "kinky kinks" and "drug capers."

The stories were untrue. Some of Elton's friends advised him to let it go; such cases were often hard to win. But Elton didn't see why anyone should get away with lying about him, and he filed suit. *The Sun* doubled down, responding to the suit with the taunting headline YOU'RE A LIAR, ELTON. The paper also continued publishing stories with further allegations of supposed bad behavior. Some of the accusations were particularly laughable. One story (bearing the headline ELTON'S SILENT ASSASSINS) alleged that he'd had his dogs' larynxes removed due to their barking. The story led to representatives from the Royal Society for the Prevention of Cruelty to Animals (RSPCA) paying Elton a visit, where they found his German shepherds in good health and their voice boxes intact.

Elton sued each time the paper published another false story, eventually racking up seventeen suits against *The Sun*. And still the stories continued. The paper eventually dredged up three Polaroids showing a naked Elton with another nude man. Though the man was not a minor or rent boy, and the photos had been taken consensually, that didn't stop the paper from blaring the headline ELTON PORN PHOTO SHAME.

Then *The Sun*'s rival, the *Daily Mirror*, came up with a true scoop, teasing the opposition with the headline ELTON THE POOF SHAFTS THE SUN. *The Sun*'s original story had cited April 30, 1986, as the date of the alleged party, and Elton always knew he had held the winning hand regarding that claim. He had not been at the home of Rod Stewart's manager dallying with rent boys, but in New York City, meeting with business associates and flying back to England at the end of the day. After relating this news to their readers, the *Mirror* then ran the story MY SEX LIES OVER ELTON, in which "Graham X" finally came clean, admitting his stories were all "all a pack of lies," and that he'd never even met Elton.

From that point on, it was only a matter of time. The day the first libel suit was due to go to the court, *The Sun* settled with Elton for £1 million in damages. The paper was also required to run its apology on the front page: SORRY ELTON, with the subhead "*Sun* pays rock star record sum." Elton's fight had won the respect of his peers, and those who deplored the sleazy tactics of tabloid media.

A big thumbs-up the day after settling *The Sun* suit, December 13, 1988.

47

BACK ON TOP AT HOME

SLEEPING WITH THE PAST

AUGUST 1989 (US RELEASE)

SEPTEMBER 1989
(UK RELEASE)

The World Tour 2, Madison Square Garden,
New York City, October 6, 1989.

Elton closed out the 1980s with his first UK #1 album in fifteen years (his last UK album chart topper being *Elton John's Greatest Hits* in 1974). It also became his bestselling album of the decade.

In an effort to cut down on the excessive partying that had marred the recording sessions of such previous albums as *Leather Jackets* (1986), Elton and Bernie opted to record at Puk Recording Studios, a converted farmhouse near the small town of Randers, Denmark, recommended by Elton's friend, George Michael. The isolated location did help the two focus on their writing, though they still found their way to the area's pubs in the evening, generously sampling the local schnapps (with Elton also flying to Paris on the weekends to hit the clubs).

Elton and Bernie decided to make the album a tribute to the R&B and soul music they'd loved while growing up that emanated from labels like Motown, Stax, and Chess. "Club at the End of the Street" has the same smooth groove of songs by the Drifters like "At the Club" and "On Broadway" (Elton had actually toured the UK with the Drifters as a backing musician during his pre-fame days). The poppy beat of the title track, a cautionary tale about not going back to a destructive relationship, clearly has its roots in the Miracles' "Shop Around." "I Never Knew Her Name" musically echoes the power of Aretha Franklin's "I Never Loved a Man," "Stone's Throw from Hurtin'" references Marvin Gaye's falsetto style, and "Amazes Me" has the sturdiness of Ray Charles's music.

Elsewhere, soul classics served more as inspirations than direct influences. Bernie had the Four Tops' "Reach Out (I'll Be There)" in mind when he wrote the lyrics to "Healing Hands," the album's standout track and its first single, but Elton's gospel-laced melody stands on its own. "Durban Deep," about the plight of miners in South Africa, might draw on Lee Dorsey's "Working in the Coalmine" thematically, but it has a decided reggae flavor. "Whispers" and "Blue Avenue" were trademark John/Taupin ballads, and the unexpected success of "Sacrifice" would help propel the album to the top.

It also marked the first time Elton didn't play an acoustic piano on record, opting instead for a Roland RD-1000 digital piano, giving the album a more contemporary sound.

Though topping the UK chart, *Sleeping with the Past* peaked at #23 in the US (it did reach the Top 10 in ten other countries). Elton so enjoyed spending such extended time with his songwriting partner, he ended up dedicating the album to Bernie. At the time of the album's release, he said, "This is probably the strongest record we've ever made. We went back to our roots and tried to do something special."

PART 4

I'M STILL STANDING, 1990–1997

48

"THE RIGORS OF ADULT LOVE"

"SACRIFICE"

MAY 1990 (UK RELEASE)

Candles in the wind. Backstage in Paris, 1990.

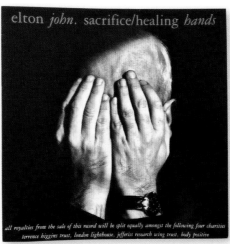

Though Elton topped the US singles chart with little difficulty (achieving five solo #1 hits in the 70s), his native country proved a tougher nut to crack; he wouldn't have a UK #1 as a solo artist until 1990 (he did have a UK #1 single in 1974 with "Don't Go Breaking My Heart," but that was a duet with Kiki Dee).

"Sacrifice," from the album *Sleeping with the Past*, is a song laced with sadness, looking at a relationship torn apart due to infidelity. "It's about a marriage falling apart and trying to live a lie when you actually can't," Bernie told *The Mail on Sunday*. "People call it the divorce song." It's one of his most personal lyrics.

In the song's video, Elton serves as an omniscient narrator, his scenes intercut with sequences of an unhappy couple, the woman turning from, and finally (on the roof of the Broadway Hollywood Building), running away from her male partner. It's a vivid depiction of living "in two separate worlds," and likely had personal resonance for both Elton and Bernie, who had each been married and divorced by this time.

Despite turning in a sensitive and emotional vocal performance, Elton was uncertain about the song and didn't want it on the album. Then, once he'd agreed it could be on, he argued against its being released as a single, feeling that with a running time of over five minutes, it would be hard to get airplay.

His assessment was partially right. On its initial release in October 1989, the song reached the Top 20 in the US, but only #55 in the UK. But over time, BBC Radio One DJ Steve Wright noticed that he was getting a strong audience response whenever he played the track. On mentioning this to the record company, it was decided to reissue the song in the UK on a double A-sided single, coupled with "Healing Hands" (another single from *Sleeping with the Past*, which had peaked at #45 in the UK). Released in May 1990, the new single sailed up the chart to #1, where it remained for five weeks. Elton donated the proceeds to various AIDS organizations; he would subsequently donate all his future earnings from his singles to charity.

By 1990, Elton's records had gone to #1 numerous times. But it must've given him great satisfaction to finally be a UK singles chart-topper in his own right.

49

"ONCE MORE, WHITE LADY— GOODBYE"

FAREWELL LETTER TO DRUGS

AUGUST 10, 1990

It was a breakup letter that was a long time coming. And this time Elton was deter-mined to see it through. He was going to overcome his drug abuse and put his other addictions behind him as well.

Elton hadn't been a big drinker during his youth, nor was he interested in drugs. His initial exposure to cocaine came about inadvertently, during his first trip to Los Angeles in 1970. He'd had dinner one night at the home of Three Dog Night's Danny Hutton and had been surprised at how energized he felt afterward. He later learned he'd been "dosed"—cocaine had been put in his food without his knowledge.

His disinterest in drugs changed in 1974, during the making of *Caribou*. He walked in on his manager John Reid snorting white powder and asked him what it was. Curious, Elton asked if he could try some. The experience wasn't pleasant; after inhaling his first line, he rushed to the bathroom to throw up, and he didn't like the numb feeling the drug left in his throat. But that didn't deter him, and cocaine became a constant companion.

Elton said he felt cocaine helped him overcome his natural shyness. And as a drug that was also popular with rock's elite, it made him feel like he was part of the in-crowd. If it led to the occasional wild night, well, excess was a part of rock 'n' roll. It's how he could blithely sing "White Lady White Powder" (from 1980's *21 at 33*), a song depicting an addict in the grip of "a habit I can't handle," and never dream that it could apply to him.

Eventually, cocaine wasn't his only problem—alcohol abuse and bulimia also plagued him. As troublesome incidents piled up, concerned friends and associates reached out to help, but he spurned their offers. The turning point came when his current boyfriend, Hugh Williams, announced he was going into rehab to deal with his own addictions. This sent Elton into a defiant downward spiral, locking himself in his bedroom, doing coke, drinking whiskey, and throwing up whatever he ate.

After two weeks, he realized that if he continued down this path, he wouldn't survive. Now he became the one to reach out, meeting with Williams and Williams's counselor. For the first time, he accepted that he was an addict and needed help.

It was an important first step, but there was a long road ahead. In rehab at Lutheran Hospital, Park Ridge (a suburb of Chicago), the man who'd had aides catering to his every whim had to learn to do basic tasks like operating a washing machine. He wrote a goodbye letter to the drug that had almost brought him to ruin, describing it as a dizzying love affair with a lethal undertow. After leaving rehab, he returned to London and put work on hold for the next year and a half, settling into what he called a "quiet routine," taking his dog for walks, going to support groups, and seeing psychiatrists.

It was a necessary period of healing. And with the newfound energy that came from being clean and sober, the years ahead were going to be increasingly productive.

At the Ritz Hotel in Paris, December 1990.

"White Lady White Powder" from 1980's 21 at 33 blithely depicted an addict in the grip of "a habit I can't handle."

50

A TRIBUTE TO LONGEVITY

TWO ROOMS:
CELEBRATING THE SONGS
OF ELTON JOHN &
BERNIE TAUPIN

OCTOBER 22, 1991
(RELEASE)

Onstage with Tina Turner at Wembley Arena, London, during her *Private Dancer* tour, March 1985. Turner would be one of several notable artists to turn up on 1991's *Two Rooms* tribute album.

TWO ROOMS
Celebrating The Songs Of
ELTON JOHN & BERNIE TAUPIN

Performed By:
Oleta Adams
The Beach Boys
Jon Bon Jovi
Kate Bush
Eric Clapton
Joe Cocker
Phil Collins
Daryl Hall & John Oates
Bruce Hornsby
George Michael
Sinead O'Connor
Rod Stewart
Sting
Tina Turner
The Who
Wilson Phillips

Given the strength of their songs, there have been numerous Elton John/Bernie Taupin tribute albums over the years. *Two Rooms* holds the distinction of being the first.

The album was a celebration of the longevity of the John/Taupin songwriting partnership. There was also the hope that the album might spark interest in their catalog, encouraging other artists to record their songs. The album's title is taken from the song "Two Rooms at the End of the World," from *21 at 33* (1980); it's also a reference to the way the two most often worked when writing a song—in separate rooms.

The album was rooted firmly in the past, all but one of the sixteen tracks from the fecund period of 1970 to 1976 (the exception was "Sacrifice" from *Sleeping with the Past*). They are among Elton's most recognizable works. But it is a surprise that songs like "I Guess That's Why They Call It the Blues," "Sad Songs

(Say So Much)," and "Nikita"—all Top 10 hits—weren't included.

There are some standout performances. Kate Bush, a longtime Elton fan, was delighted to be asked to participate. Her reggae-influenced "Rocket Man" was released in the UK, reaching #12; the B-side had her cover of another Elton John song that didn't appear on *Two Rooms*, "Candle in the Wind." Oleta Adams's heartfelt rendition of "Don't Let the Sun Go Down on Me" reached #33 in the UK, while Rod Stewart's "Your Song" was pleasant, if not particularly distinguished, which perhaps explains its chart performance, peaking at #41 in both the US and UK.

Tina Turner's "The Bitch Is Back" is another standout. Already a highlight of her live show, it's a track she has great fun with. Elton's friend George Michael gives a wonderfully sensitive performance of "Tonight," and Sinead O'Connor's performance of "Sacrifice" is stunningly beautiful.

But it's also an uneven album, described as a "mixed bag" in *Billboard*. Most critics gave a thumbs down to Jon Bon Jovi's somewhat overwrought version of "Levon." Bruce Hornsby's "Madman Across the Water" and Phil Collins's "Burn Down the Mission" also weren't rated very highly.

But overall, the successes outweighed the occasional misfires. The jazzy touch Sting brings to "Come Down in Time" is another highlight. And record buyers were receptive; the album reached #18 in the US, and #1 on the UK's Top 20 Compilation Albums chart. Overall, a good showcase of the best of Elton's and Bernie's 1970s work, as interpreted by top contemporary artists.

51

"IT WAS AN AMAZING FRIENDSHIP"

"DON'T LET THE SUN GO DOWN ON ME" WITH GEORGE MICHAEL

NOVEMBER 25, 1991 (RELEASE)

"Don't Let the Sun Go Down on Me" was one of the best tracks on Elton's *Caribou* album. But it didn't become a chart-topper until almost twenty years after its initial release.

It's one of the most dramatic numbers in Elton's catalog, a song of yearning from someone trying to mend a faltering relationship. Elton has always said it was meant as his tribute to the Beach Boys, an influence you can hear most strongly in the backing vocals on the chorus (which featured two actual Beach Boys among the vocalists, Carl Wilson and Bruce Johnston). The Tower of Power horn section further added to the song's anthemic sweep.

But Elton had problems recording a satisfactory vocal, becoming so frustrated at one point that he told producer Gus Dudgeon the song should be given to Engelbert Humperdinck, "and if he doesn't want it, tell him to send it to Lulu!" Even after finishing the song, he still hated it and didn't want it on the album. He was eventually persuaded otherwise and was rewarded with another hit when it was released as a single, reaching #2 in the US, #16 in the UK.

When Elton had Wham! perform with him at Live Aid in 1985, George Michael took the lead on "Don't Let the Sun. . ." while his partner Andrew Ridgeley sang backing vocals. It marked the beginning of Michael's friendship with Elton. Michael soon sang backing vocals on Elton's 1985 album, *Ice on Fire*. The following year, Elton made a surprise appearance at Wham!'s final concert at Wembley Stadium, dressed as Ronald McDonald.

Michael invited Elton to make a guest appearance during the last show of his *Cover to Cover* tour on March 23, 1991, at Wembley Arena, to revisit "Don't Let the Sun. . . ." This time they sang the song together, Elton coming in after the first chorus. But when he learned that Michael wanted to release the song as a single, Elton advised against it, thinking it wasn't strong enough. He was proved wrong when the single topped the charts not only in the US and UK, but in five other countries as well. Proceeds were donated to charity. It would be Michael's last #1 single.

While the video for the song features audio from the March 1991 performance, the film footage is actually from Michael's October 20, 1991, concert in Rosemont, Illinois.

There were rocky periods in their friendship. When Elton reached out to

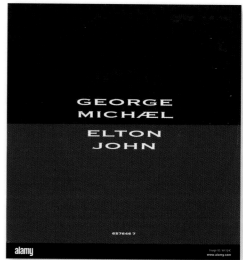

With George Michael backstage Wembley, July 13, 1985.

help his friend address his substance abuse, Michael hit back, telling *The Guardian*, "He will not be happy until I bang on his door in the middle of the night saying, 'Please, please, help me, Elton. Take me to rehab.' It's not going to happen.... Elton just needs to shut his mouth and get on with his own life." The two eventually became friendly again.

George Michael was found dead at his home in Oxfordshire on December 25, 2016, at age fifty-three. His death was attributed to problems with his heart and liver. Elton posted a photo of the two on his Instagram page, writing, "I am in deep shock. I have lost a beloved friend—the kindest, most generous soul and a brilliant artist. My heart goes out to his family, friends and all of his fans."

52

"WE ARE THE CHAMPIONS"

Performing with Axl Rose at the Freddie Mercury Tribute Concert.

THE FREDDIE MERCURY TRIBUTE

APRIL 20, 1992

There was no question that Elton would appear on the bill of the Freddie Mercury Tribute concert, a benefit performance that commemorated Queen's flamboyant lead singer, who'd died the previous year at age forty-five. Proceeds from the show were used to launch the AIDS charity the Mercury Phoenix Trust.

Elton and Mercury had been friends for years. John Reid had managed Queen for a short time in the 1970s when the band broke through to international acclaim—which might not have happened had Reid listened to Elton's advice about "Bohemian Rhapsody." On hearing an advance pressing of the single, Elton told Reid not to release it; it was far too over the top to be successful. Sales of over ten million copies proved him quite wrong.

Mercury delighted Elton. He was smart and funny, and had a penchant for excess that matched Elton's own. "Freddie Mercury could out-party me, which is saying something," he told *Uncut* magazine. "His appetites were

unquenchable." A number of Elton's friends had drag names—Elton was Sharon, Rod Stewart was Phyllis, John Reid was Beryl—and Mercury joined in, taking the name Melina after Greek actress Melina Mercouri.

When Mercury was diagnosed with AIDS, he kept the news to himself for a

THE
FREDDIE MERCURY
TRIBUTE

SOLD OUT
THANK YOU ALL

CONCERT FOR AIDS AWARENESS
Profits to Aids Charities Worldwide

EASTER MONDAY APRIL 20th 1992
WEMBLEY STADIUM
Gates open 3.30pm   Show starts 6.00pm   Show finishes approx. 9.00pm

General Admission £25
A limited number of Reserved Seats at £30 and £35 available only by calling 081 862 0202
Personal callers welcome at Wembley Box Office and at Virgin Megastore Oxford St. & Marble Arch
also Allders of Croydon, Allders of Sutton, Bentalls of Kingston, and all branches of Keith Prowse
CREDIT CARD HOTLINES
Wembley Stadium 081 900 1234 / 071 240 7200 / 071 379 6131 / 071 836 4114
071 734 8932 / 071 580 3141
Limit of 6 tickets per person
(All tickets subject to booking fee except for personal callers at Wembley Box Office)
INFORMATION LINE (0891) 500 255 calls charged at 36p cheap rate, 48p other times

Concert produced by Queen and Harvey Goldsmith Entertainments

long time; even his bandmates weren't told at first. Elton learned of Mercury's illness through friends and made frequent visits to Mercury's home during his final weeks. He later said he found the visits painful, as his old friend's body was so ravaged by the disease. Yet in his up moments, Mercury was still eager to share another bit of gossip, in between placing bids on items he saw in auction catalogs.

Mercury died on November 24, 1991. Elton attended his funeral service on November 27. That Christmas, he opened his door to receive an unexpected gift: a painting by Henry Scott Tuke that Mercury had purchased for him at an auction, accompanied by a note: "Darling Sharon—thought you'd love this. Love, Melina."

Queen's guitarist Brian May and drummer Roger Taylor announced the upcoming charity concert at the BRIT Awards in February 1992. The show was held at Wembley Stadium, the site of Queen's triumphant appearance at Live Aid in 1985, where they were generally

Elton opened his set seated at the piano, singing the song he'd once disparaged, "Bohemian Rhapsody."

regarded as having stolen the show. The show opened with short sets by Metallica, Def Leppard, and Spinal Tap, among others. Then Queen took the stage and backed a revolving succession of performers, including Robert Plant, David Bowie, George Michael, and Annie Lennox.

Elton, wearing black leather trousers, black cowboy boots, and a red fringed jacket with gold trim, opened his set seated at the piano, singing the song he'd once disparaged, "Bohemian Rhapsody." Elton performed the opening ballad section, footage from the song's original video played during the operatic section, and Guns N' Roses' Axl Rose sang the hard rock section, Elton joining him on the song's outro. Elton then gave a highly emotional performance of one of the last songs Mercury wrote, "The Show Must Go On," coming downstage to sing, using a cordless mike.

"Elton's a good old cookie, isn't he?" Mercury's quoted as saying in *Freddie Mercury: His Life, In His Own Words*. "I love him to death and I think he's fabulous." As Elton put it in the note that accompanied the floral tribute he'd sent to Mercury's funeral, "Thank you for being my friend. I will love you always."

The flowers Elton sent to Mercury's funeral.

53

"NOW I'VE GOT TO GIVE SOMETHING BACK"

THE FIRST ELTON JOHN AIDS FOUNDATION OSCAR-VIEWING PARTY

MARCH 29, 1993

The Elizabeth Taylor AIDS Foundation concert, Madison Square Garden, New York City, October 11, 1992.

Once he got clean and sober, Elton greatly expanded his charitable work in the fight against AIDS.

Over the years, he'd played benefits for AIDS causes and appeared on the "That's What Friends Are For" charity single, organized by Dionne Warwick and credited to "Dionne & Friends" (released in October 1985, the single raised over $3 million). But he considered that work minimal. "I didn't do enough," he later told *Vanity Fair*. "I wasn't at the forefront as a gay man."

During this same time, he'd come to know Ryan White, a teenager living in Kokomo, Indiana, who'd contracted AIDS from a blood transfusion. When his school tried to ban him from returning to class, his plight became national news. Due to harassment and death threats, the family moved to Cicero, Indiana.

Word reached Elton that White liked his music, so when he next toured the States, he invited White and his family to Los Angeles to see one of his shows; they later visited Disneyland. Elton kept in touch afterward. "He just became part of our family," White's mother Jeanne explained. He was one of those at White's side when he died and served as one of his pallbearers. Inspired by the example of White and his family in promoting AIDS awareness, he announced he would give the proceeds from every future single he released to AIDS charities.

In 1992, he founded the Elton John AIDS Foundation (EJAF), selling his record collection (forty-six thousand singles, twenty thousand albums) for startup funds. In the words of the organization's website, the foundation "funds frontline partners to prevent infections, fight stigma and provide treatment with love, compassion and dignity for the most vulnerable groups affected by HIV around the world."

Elton struck up a friendship with Ryan White, an Indiana teenager who'd contracted AIDS from a blood transfusion.

One of the longest-running fundraisers for the EJAF was an annual Oscar party. The first event was organized when the foundation teamed up with Patrick Lippert, executive director of the voter registration group Rock the Vote, who always held a fundraising Oscar party for different causes. After being diagnosed with AIDS himself, he wanted to do a fundraiser for that cause. The 1993 party, held at Dudley Moore's Maple Drive Restaurant in Beverly Hills, drew 140 attendees, and raised $350,000. Sadly, Lippert died three weeks after the event.

The annual party attracted a star-studded roster of attendees. At 1994's event, Elton was photographed in a booth with Steven Spielberg, Tom Hanks, Bruce Springsteen, and his wife Patti Scialfa. The size and scope grew as it became a must-do event. "People have to go to other parties, but people *want* to go to Elton's party," said Sharon Stone, who donated her car for one of the party's auctions. After some persuasion, Elton began performing a few songs at the party before introducing new performers—Nelly Furtado, John Legend, and Ed Sheeran have all put in appearances.

The EJAF has now raised over $400 million since its inception. Elton's memoir, *Love Is the Cure: On Life, Loss, and the End of AIDS*, published in 2012, tells more about his AIDS charity work.

The "That's What Friends Are For" charity single was organized by Dionne Warwick and credited to "Dionne & Friends."

54

A HALL OF FAMER

ELTON'S INDUCTION IN THE ROCK HALL

JANUARY 19, 1994

Elton and Bernie after the Hall of Fame induction. "Without Bernie, there wouldn't have been any Elton John at all," Elton stated in his acceptance speech.

Attendees who watched Elton John inducted into the Rock and Roll Hall of Fame don't know how lucky they were. For Elton came close to not appearing at all.

The Rock and Roll Hall of Fame was established in 1983 as the forerunner of a museum that would honor influential figures in the rock music industry, primarily musicians and singers, but also nonperformers (songwriters,

producers, DJs). A performer becomes eligible for induction twenty-five years after the release of their first record.

It wasn't the first time Elton participated at a Rock Hall function. In 1988, he inducted the Beach Boys, and in 2011 he'd induct another musician he admired, Leon Russell. But when he was inducted himself, he admitted he had mixed feelings about the Rock Hall, twenty-five years after the release of

"I've Been Loving You." Thinking it had become too commercial an enterprise, he considered turning down the honor. One reason he accepted was because Axl Rose would be inducting him, and he considered Rose a friend.

Nonetheless, when he first arrived at the Waldorf, where the ceremony would be held, with his boyfriend David Furnish, he abruptly changed his mind about participating and went back to his hotel. Then he felt bad about leaving and returned in time to see the Grateful Dead inducted alongside a life-size cutout of Jerry Garcia, who'd declined to attend. This reconfirmed Elton's own desire to not participate and he departed once again. He returned to his hotel only to come back to the Waldorf once more—and depart again before returning. His memoir even hints that there may have been yet another return, departure, and return to the Waldorf.

Seymour Stein, president of the Rock Hall's board of directors and the co-founder of Sire Records, made some opening remarks, introducing a short film about Elton. Rose then made his brief remarks, admitting he felt a little out of his depth and was going to keep things simple. "For myself, as well as many others, no one has been there more for inspiration than Elton John," he said, going on to note that he placed Elton and Bernie in the same pantheon of great rock duos as John Lennon and Paul McCartney and Mick Jagger and Keith Richards. "When I first heard 'Bennie and the Jets,' I knew at that time that I had to be a performer," he concluded, before introducing Elton.

Elton referenced a number of his influences, not only Little Richard and Jerry Lee Lewis, but also his childhood favorite Winifred Atwell and British pianist George Shearing. He credited rock 'n' roll with enlivening his "boring fucking childhood," and in a gracious

gesture, called Bernie on stage and handed him the award. "Without Bernie, there wouldn't have been any Elton John at all," he explained.

He was equally humble backstage, telling one journalist, "You know, anyone can make it if they try." It was a calm moment in what had been a rather fraught evening. On their way back to the hotel, Furnish turned to his boyfriend and said, "Elton, is your life *always* like this?"

55

"I JUST CAN'T WAIT TO BE KING"

With *Lion King* lyricist Tim Rice. "Can You Feel the Love Tonight" took home the Oscar for Best Original Song.

THE LION KING

**JUNE 12, 1994
(WORLD PREMIERE)**

The Lion King was a hit film. Then it became a phenomenon. In addition to spawning sequels, two television series, video games, a stage musical, and a remake, it also took Elton in a new creative direction.

Elton had first written with lyricist Tim Rice in the late 70s; their song, "Legal Boys," appeared on Elton's 1982 album *Jump Up!* Rice had shot to fame in the 1970s with the musicals he'd written with Andrew Lloyd Webber, *Jesus Christ Superstar* and *Evita*. After writing songs with composer Alan Menken for Disney's animated musical *Aladdin* (1992), he was asked to contribute to *The Lion King*. Menken was unavailable for the project, as was ABBA's Benny Andersson, with whom Rice had collaborated on the

musical *Chess* (1985). Rice then suggested Elton as a collaborator.

Elton had previously written soundtrack music for the 1970 film *Friends*. Though the film received mixed reviews, the soundtrack album edged into the Top 40 due to Elton's name. But it wasn't a realm he felt totally comfortable in, and later admitted that even after agreeing to Rice's offer he still had doubts about the venture.

Elton enjoyed working with his new songwriting partner; Rice wrote his lyrics first and passed them on to Elton, just like Bernie did. It also reminded Elton of how the songs had come together for *Captain Fantastic*, following a designated storyline.

The two wrote five songs for the film. "Circle of Life," about the interconnectedness of all living creatures, is the stirring opening number. "I Just Can't Wait to Be King" establishes the essential good nature of the youthful lion Simba. "Be Prepared" is a darkly comic number for Simba's wicked uncle Scar, who plots to take over the kingdom. "Hakuna Matata" is the catchy, cheerful anthem by Simba's friends, Timon (a meerkat) and Pumbaa (a warthog), meaning "no worries"—"our problem-free philosophy," they explain. "Can You Feel the Love Tonight" is ostensibly a love song between Simba and his mate Nala, but has an amusing lyrical counterpoint, as Timon fears their romance will curtail his friendship with Simba. The film's score was composed by Hans Zimmer.

The Lion King was a smash on its release, becoming the highest-grossing film of 1994, the highest-grossing film of the Walt Disney Animation Studios, and the highest-grossing animated film of all time, a record it held until the release of Captain Nemo in 2003. Three of its songs received Oscar nominations for Best Original Song; "Can You Feel the Love Tonight" took home the honor.

The film's soundtrack was just as successful, topping charts in the US and four other countries. It sold over ten million copies in the US, making it the bestselling soundtrack from an animated film, and over eighteen million copies worldwide. Elton's solo performance of "Can You Feel the Love Tonight," which played over the film's closing credits, won the Grammy for Best Male Pop Vocal Performance.

And that was just the beginning. In 1997, The Lion King became a stage musical, opening on Broadway on October 15. Director Julie Taymor made the show a visual delight with her imaginative use of elaborate masks and large puppets operated by the actors; the Broadway

THE GREATEST ADVENTURE OF ALL
IS FINDING OUR PLACE
IN THE CIRCLE OF LIFE.

WALT DISNEY PICTURES
presents
THE
LION KING

production won six Tony Awards, including Best Musical. Elton and Rice contributed three additional songs for the show, "The Morning Report" (which had actually been written for the film but was cut), "The Madness of King Scar," and "Chow Down," sung by hungry hyenas.

The movie was remade as a "photorealistic computer-animated film" in 2019, with Elton reworking some elements of his original music; he and Rice also wrote a new song, "Never Too Late," which plays over the closing credits. The film was another huge success, and currently holds the record

as highest-grossing animated film of all time. But while a great technological achievement, the remake lacks the charm and humor of the 1994 film. Elton was also unhappy with it, telling GQ magazine it was "a huge disappointment to me. . . . The magic and joy were lost."

Nonetheless, The Lion King set the stage for Elton's future successes with musicals.

56

DUELING PIANOS

THE *FACE TO FACE* TOUR WITH BILLY JOEL

JULY 8–AUGUST 21, 1994

Elton and Billy Joel greet the audience at the Meadowlands, East Rutherford, New Jersey, July 22, 1994.

It was a natural matchup. Elton John and Billy Joel were the most successful piano players in the pop realm, having between them a staggering number of hits. What could be more obvious than sending them out on the road together?

The first such tour was relatively short, just twenty-one dates, and all of them in the US. The opening night setlist, July 8, 1994, at Veterans Stadium in Philadelphia (still a hot and humid 93 degrees when the concert began at 8:00 p.m.) set the template for their subsequent tours. The shows would open with Elton and Billy performing a few songs together (on that first night, the three numbers were Elton's "Your Song" and "Don't Let the Sun Go Down on Me" and Billy's "Honesty"). Then each performer did a set of their own, alternating the order in which they went on throughout the tour. They joined up again at the end, playing pianos facing each other, for a final set of their own numbers, plus a few covers thrown in for fun (the first concert featured a run of

50s and 60s classics: the Beatles' "A Hard Day's Night," Little Richard's "Lucille," and Jerry Lee Lewis's "Great Balls of Fire"). And after opening the show with an Elton song, it was only fitting that it closed with one of Billy's: his signature number "Piano Man." Author Elisabeth Rosenthal cited the song's performance at the debut show as "turning Veterans Stadium into a colossal piano bar and encouraging the most spirited sing-along of the night."

What made the shows especially fun was when each performer added a cover of his co-star's songs to his own set. Audiences were tickled to hear Elton perform Billy's "New York State of Mind," while Billy took on Elton's "Goodbye Yellow Brick Road." Fans cited such moments as particular highlights. The two musicians also made guest appearances during each other's set, Billy coming on to join Elton in singing "I Guess That's Why They Call It the Blues," for example.

The first *Face to Face* tour was wildly successful, selling out every date and getting positive reviews. For the next fifteen years, John/Joel tours were a regular occurrence, but over time, a strain began to show. In his review of a 2009 performance in St. Louis, *Riverfront Times* critic Christian Schaeffer observed, "Watching the show, one didn't get the impression that the two men are especially good friends or even great admirers of each other's work," and felt they only "came alive" when they played their solo sets. Further disagreements arose when

Elton went public with his concern about Billy's drinking, claiming it led to Joel pulling out of a planned 2010 summer tour. Billy responded that he'd never signed off on the tour to begin with and was unable to go out on the road due to hip surgery.

The two sparred in the press for a while, but eventually patched up their differences. Nonetheless, there have been no further John/Joel tours.

Busch Stadium, St. Louis, Missouri, August 9, 1994. The first *Face to Face* tour was wildly successful, selling out every date and getting positive reviews.

57

A PEEP AT THE INNER SANCTUM

TANTRUMS & TIARAS
DOCUMENTARY

JULY 7, 1996
(UK BROADCAST)

Elton John Aids Foundation event at The Georgian Terrace Hotel, Atlanta, Georgia, May 29, 1996. Some fans were shocked by the frankness that Furnish presented in the documentary.

It wasn't unusual for Elton to be followed around by cameras when he was on tour. But the footage captured as Elton made yet another jaunt around the world in 1995 would be used for a documentary that was unlike any he had participated in before.

Elton had been approached about making a documentary but he wasn't interested in the kind of standard celebrity profile that he considered "a load of whitewashed bullshit." He wanted someone whom he trusted to make it, someone whom he felt comfortable opening up to. So his partner David Furnish became the film's director, Elton joking that it was Furnish's way of showing everybody what he had to put up with.

The film is primarily about Elton's working life. He's seen promoting his latest album, making a video, accepting his Oscar for *The Lion King*, and performing (most of the footage drawn from a concert in Rio de Janeiro). He's most in his element when he's performing, aside from one uncomfortable moment during a concert in Santiago—offstage while Ray Cooper solos on percussion, he's unable to catch his breath and seems on the verge of a heart attack. But when he's out of the spotlight, he's unable to relax, admitting that his "tunnel vision" in a year full of touring has him always looking ahead to the next gig.

It's the behind-the-scenes moments that are the most revealing. Furnish describes their world as being like "a medieval court," and indeed it does seem as if Elton lives in a cloistered world. Aside from Elton's mother and grandmother, the only people he's seen interacting with are staff. But he lets his guard down with Furnish, looking into the camera unselfconsciously, answering whatever question is put to him. Interestingly, though his life revolves around music, there's little discussion about his work beyond his casually mentioning that he rarely takes more than an hour to write a song.

Though it's been referred to as a "warts and all" documentary, the "tantrum" sequences are rather restrained. The only time Elton is seen in an explosive mood is when he's seen ranting about an aide leaving behind the clothes he needs to wear for a video shoot. Otherwise, we see the moments after the explosion, as when Elton walks off a tennis court while on vacation. It takes him three days to explain what upset him: a woman waving at him while he was playing.

The most pointed look at his behavior comes when Furnish shows him footage of a conversation between himself and Elton's therapist, Beechy Colclough. The therapist pulls no punches, calling Elton "a totally addictive, compulsive person" with low self-esteem. Though Elton bristles at being so "picked over," he concedes a lot of the assessment is "extremely accurate."

Some friends, and viewers, were shocked at the film's frankness. But Elton didn't mind not being shown at his best because he felt it made the film more real. Though he did regret its leading to the deluge of reality TV programs about celebrities like the Kardashians, "for which I can only prostrate myself before the human race and beg their forgiveness."

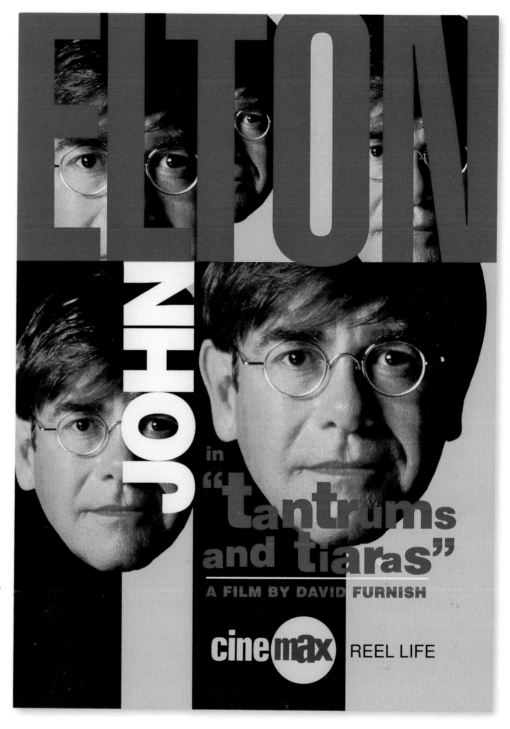

ELTON JOHN in "tantrums and tiaras"

A FILM BY DAVID FURNISH

cinemax REEL LIFE

58

"GOODBYE, ENGLAND'S ROSE"

MEMORIAL PERFORMANCE OF "CANDLE IN THE WIND"

SEPTEMBER 6, 1997

Elton John performed a revised version of "Candle in the Wind" at the funeral of Diana, Princess of Wales, at Westminster Abbey, London, September 6, 1997.

The sudden death of Princess Diana in a car accident in Paris on August 31, 1997, stunned the world. Elton was particularly distraught. He'd known the Princess for over fifteen years, and had just seen her the previous month, at the funeral of their friend Gianni Versace.

The two had met in 1981, just prior to Lady Diana Spencer's marriage to Prince Charles, when Elton and Ray Cooper had been asked to provide entertainment for Prince Andrew's twenty-first birthday party at Windsor Castle. Elton and Diana hit it off straightaway and ended up dancing the Charleston together. They went on to be good friends, and he particularly admired her charity work.

Then the two had a falling out over Versace's Rock and Royalty book, which featured photographs of musicians and royals wearing Versace finery. Diana wrote a foreword for the book, but then withdrew it, due to the book's racier photographs, which she claimed she

hadn't seen in advance. Elton wrote her an angry letter and the two stopped speaking. They made up when she telephoned Elton after Versace's murder.

Now, just over six weeks later, Diana herself was dead. There are varying accounts of how "Candle in the Wind" came to be rewritten in her honor. According to Elton's memoir, he was approached by entrepreneur Richard Branson, speaking on behalf of Diana's family. UK radio stations had been playing "Candle in the Wind" in tribute to Diana, and mourners who visited St. James's Palace, where her coffin lay in the Royal Chapel, were leaving quotations from the song in the chapel's book of condolence. Would Bernie agree to rewrite the song's lyrics for Elton to sing at the funeral at Westminster Abbey on September 6? They readily agreed, and the song was reworked.

Elton was understandably nervous about performing the song, with new lyrics he'd barely had time to rehearse,

live in front of a worldwide audience. But his performance was magnificent, the emotion clearly evident in his voice. He later recalled being so caught up in the moment he had few specific memories of his performance, only of the response afterward, when applause from the mourners outside seemed to "sweep into the church itself."

Later, he went to Townhouse Studios where producer George Martin was waiting, to record a studio version of the song. Elton recorded two takes live at the piano, then overdubbed a harmony vocal. Martin added a string quartet and a woodwind player. Though not evincing the rawer emotion of the live version, it was a tasteful, sensitive rendition.

"Something About the Way You Look Tonight" was already planned as a single to promote Elton's latest album, The Big Picture. Now a revised single was released, with "Candle in the Wind 1997" joining "Something . . ." on the A-side, and "You Can Make History (Young Again)" on the B-side. All proceeds were earmarked for the Diana, Princess of Wales Memorial Fund.

Sales surpassed everybody's expectations. It sold 1.5 million copies in the UK in the first week, eventually becoming the country's bestselling single of all time. It topped the charts in twenty-one countries, with worldwide sales of over thirty-three million. Even albums that featured the original version of the song enjoyed a bump in sales.

But the constant news reports over the single's success came to bother Elton, who felt it encouraged a "wallowing" in Diana's death. He never performed the new version live again, and even stopped performing the original version for a while. "Candle in the Wind 1997" remains of its time, a heartfelt tribute to a friend.

PART 5

NATIONAL TREASURE, 1998– PRESENT

59

ARISE, SIR ELTON

IN WHICH ELTON HERCULES JOHN BECOMES A KNIGHT OF THE REALM

FEBRUARY 24, 1998

At one time, it was controversial to award a knighthood to an entertainer, but by the 1990s, numerous performers had received such honors.

"They don't come any bigger than this," was Elton's comment to the press after being knighted by his queen and proudly displaying his medal for photographers. It was certainly an indication of how far he'd come from his humble beginnings in Pinner.

It was not Elton's first royal honor. In 1996, he was made Commander of the Order of the British Empire (CBE), "For services to music and for charitable services." At one time, it was controversial to award an honor to a mere entertainer; when The Beatles had received the Member of the Order of the British Empire (MBE) in 1965, several other recipients returned their medals in protest. But by the 1990s, numerous performers had received such honors, particularly if they were heavily involved in charity work.

Then in 1997, it was announced that Elton would receive a knighthood, "For services to music and charitable services." Elton credited his hard-won sobriety for his dedication to charitable works in the 1990s, adding, "A knighthood is the icing on the cake."

A respectful Elton had no intention of upstaging the monarch at the investiture at Buckingham Palace, wearing a formal black suit with white shirt, gray waistcoat, and gray tie. His partner David Furnish was also in attendance, as well as his mother and stepfather.

As he approached Queen Elizabeth, Lord Camoys, the Lord Chamberlain, mistakenly announced him as "Sir John Elton." But the rest of the ceremony adhered to convention, Elton placing one knee on a stool and bowing his head, the Queen then tapping him on each shoulder with the knighting sword used by her father, George VI, as Colonel of the Scots Guards.

The two chatted briefly afterward. "Her Majesty said she hoped being here today didn't interfere too much with my arrangements," he said following the ceremony. "She said I must be terribly busy." In fact, Elton was in the midst of touring, and had flown back from the US only the day before; on February 26, he'd be off to Australia for the next leg of the tour. "But there was no way I would miss this."

"I am extremely proud," he added. "I love my country and to be recognized in such a way—I can't think of anything better."

In 2020, Elton received an additional honor: being made Companion of the Order of the Companions of Honour (CH), "For services to music and to charity." It's an award given to those of exceptional accomplishment, and there can be no more than sixty-five Companions at any one time.

With mother Sheila Farebrother, partner David Furnish, his stepfather Fred Farebrother after receiving his knighthood in London, February 24, 1998.

60

"SKY'S THE LIMIT"

**BACKING A SPACE
SHUTTLE LAUNCH**

OCTOBER 29, 1998

The original 1972 release of "Rocket Man" coincided with NASA's Apollo 16 mission, which the record company referenced in ads for the single.

Elton offered a live performance of "Rocket Man" at the October 29, 1998, launch of the Space Shuttle, shown here.

The weather at Florida's Kennedy Space Center was perfect for the launch of the Space Shuttle *Discovery* on the sunny morning of October 29, 1998. Mission STS-95 had Senator John Glenn as a crewmember for Glenn's first return to space since his historic 1962 flight, when he became the first American to orbit the Earth (Glenn, at age seventy-seven, would become the then-oldest person to go into space). President Bill Clinton and his wife Hillary were both on hand to witness the event. And so was Elton, who was asked to provide some highly appropriate music for the event: a live performance of the song "Rocket Man (I Think It's Going to Be a Long, Long Time)."

The song dated back to 1972. As Bernie was driving to visit his parents one evening, the first lines came to him. In some accounts, he saw a light in the sky, either an airplane or a shooting star, during his drive. He raced to his parents' home, repeating the lines so he wouldn't forget them, then rushed inside, saying, "Please don't anyone talk to me until I've written this down!" The melancholy ballad about an alienated astronaut ("It's lonely out in space") drew immediate comparisons with David Bowie's similarly themed "Space Oddity," not least because the two songs shared the same producer, Gus Dudgeon. But

Bernie always denied there was any connection, though he did say he took the title from a song with the same name by Florida band Pearls Before Swine (who cited Ray Bradbury's short story "The Rocket Man" as their inspiration).

Following its release in April 1972, the single reached #6 in the US, #2 in the UK. In a nice bit of timing, the release coincided with NASA's Apollo 16 mission, which the record company referenced in ads for the single: "What a trip! Both launchings bound to set new records." Elton, then on tour in the States, was invited to visit NASA's Houston, Texas, facility, along with Bernie and the band. Al Worden, the command module pilot of the Apollo 15 mission, was the group's escort as they examined artifacts, and each took a turn in the flight simulator.

Kate Bush recorded a cover of the song for the 1991 tribute compilation *Two Rooms*; released as a single, it reached #12 in the UK chart. Portuguese singer David Fonseca had a Top 20 hit with the song in 2007. But the most notorious cover was William Shatner's performance on the Science Fiction Film Awards (aka the 5th Saturn Awards), held on January 14, 1978. Clad in a black suit, dress shirt, and black bowtie, *Star Trek*'s Captain Kirk gave a

spoken-word recitation of the song in his inimitable style, as if reciting a sonnet by Shakespeare (and underscoring the meaning of the line "And I'm gonna be high" while smoking what was presumably a cigarette). A more gravelly-voiced rendition can be found on Shatner's 2011 album, *Seeking Major Tom*.

Elton was given an official NASA orange jumpsuit on the occasion of the *Discovery* launch performance, which he signed in silver ink. Most recently, the song was referenced in the remix of "Cold Heart" on Elton's 2021 album *The Lockdown Sessions*.

61

ALMOST FAMOUS REVIVES AN OLD SINGLE

"TINY DANCER"

SEPTEMBER 8, 2000
(WORLD PREMIERE)

The cast of Cameron Crowe's *Almost Famous*.
The film gave "Tiny Dancer" a second life.

Cameron Crowe's *Almost Famous* was a love letter to the classic rock of the 1970s. And whose music embodied the breezy tunefulness of the decade better than Elton's?

"Tiny Dancer" is a concise summary of Elton's and Bernie's first trip to the US—driving down the road late at night, meeting "Jesus freaks" hanging out on the street, standing backstage while watching the "piano man" strut his hour upon the stage. And there's a special lyrical nod to the band's seamstress, who's destined to marry a "music man." It's a reference to Bernie's first wife, Maxine Feibelman, whom he met in LA on that first trip. She joined their entourage and did quick repairs of the band's stage wear, going on to marry Bernie in 1971. The music, which starts out quietly then builds over the course of the six-minute song, sweeps the listener up in the delirious excitement of finding a new love to go along with one's new life.

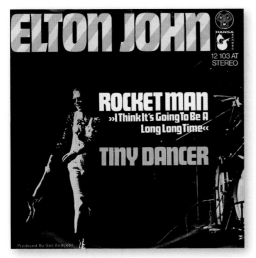

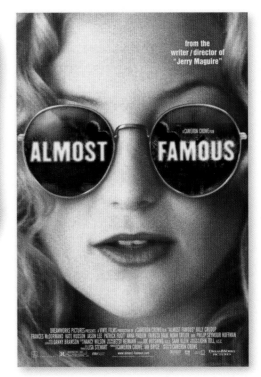

The song appeared on *Madman Across the Water* and was released as a single, peaking at #41 in the US, though it hit the Top 20 in Canada and Australia (it wasn't released as a single in the UK). It nonetheless made its way into Elton's setlists. It also made its first film appearance in 1975's *Aloha, Bobby and Rose*.

Almost Famous, which premiered at the Toronto International Film Festival in September 2000 and is loosely based on Crowe's life, is the story of a budding rock journalist (William Miller, played by Patrick Fugit) endeavoring to write his first big story about a fictional rock band, Stillwater. There was only one sentence in the script about how "Tiny Dancer" would be used in the film, when the band is traveling on their tour bus: "They listen to 'Tiny Dancer' on the bus and sing along as Russell [Stillwater's lead guitarist, played by Billy Crudup] realizes the warmth of the community of his band and crew."

But the sequence turned out to be so much more. The band members are seen sitting quietly on the bus, recovering from the hard partying of the night before. "Tiny Dancer" comes on the radio, and one by one they join in singing the song. It's a moment of joyful camaraderie that draws the audience in as well, a wonderful moment illustrating the unifying power of music. "It was like a physical thing when they started singing along, and you could feel all the relationships in that one spot," Crowe told *Rolling Stone*. "They're singing, and you just can't help but go: 'This is the movie! This is everything!'"

On seeing the film, people immediately recognized the sequence as a key moment in the film—including Elton, whose response to Crowe on watching it was, "I always loved that song, 'Tiny Dancer.' You *understand* that song 'Tiny Dancer'!"

"And he started playing it in his show and he's never stopped playing it. He gives us credit for it," Crowe proudly noted.

And so *Almost Famous* reawakened interest in a song that otherwise might've remained a lesser-known single. Indeed, when Elton performs it in concert, it's the film that likely comes to mind.

62

ROCKING THE HIGH ROLLERS

FIRST LAS VEGAS RESIDENCY

FEBRUARY 13, 2004
(OPENING NIGHT)

In 2004, Elton found an unexpected home in the city that never sleeps: Las Vegas.

When Elton was offered the chance to do a Vegas residency, his first instinct was to turn it down. For years, Las Vegas's showbiz glitz had seemed the antithesis of the wild, free-spirited unconventionality of rock 'n' roll. Las Vegas meant middle-of-the-road entertainment like Wayne Newton, or, for the more sophisticated, spending an hour with the Rat Pack, watching Frank and Dino and Sammy trading quips and songs. That began to change with Elvis Presley's first Vegas residency in 1969, which injected a welcome dose of youthful energy into the scene. And by the twenty-first century, rockers and rappers alike were adding a Vegas stop to their touring itineraries; the Hard Rock Cafe even opened their own casino/hotel in the city.

Elton himself had played Vegas numerous times over the years, beginning with the Convention Center in 1971. By 2004, he realized that he didn't have to do a standard Vegas production; he had the freedom to do whatever he wanted with his show, which would be called *The Red Piano*. He brought in filmmaker/photographer David LaChapelle to direct and design the production, telling him to "let his imagination run riot."

And so he did. "Director David LaChapelle has managed to cram almost every popular cliche about Las Vegas onto the 22,500-square-foot stage of The Colosseum at Caesars Palace," wrote Jerry Fink in his review for the *Las Vegas Sun*. "The production is tacky, trashy, glitzy, neon-heavy, hyperbolic and possibly the most entertaining show in town." Fink described a stage "littered" with neon signs and large phallic bananas, lipstick tubes, hot dogs, and ice cream cones,

as well as inflatable roses that "grow to the size of elephants." He also noted the copious semi-nudity in the films LaChapelle created as the backdrop to the songs, largely drawn from Elton's 70s catalog. "Don't Let the Sun Go Down on Me" featured a couple doing a sensual dance around their living room; "The Bitch Is Back" featured a pole-dancing Pamela Anderson. The show's most subdued element? Elton himself, simply attired in a series of black suits with colorful shirts.

Though Elton's mother took exception to the show's racier antics, audiences loved it, and what was initially a seventy-five-show run was extended to 247 shows. *The Red Piano* finally closed on March 22, 2009. Elton took an abbreviated version of the show overseas (*The Red Piano: Live in Europe*) in 2008 and 2009, following a single warmup date in London. The show was also released on CD and DVD/Blu-ray.

The production was deemed such a success, Elton returned to Vegas with a new show, *The Million Dollar Piano*, which opened at Caesars on February 19, 2011, and ran through May 17, 2018 (the show's name referred to a custom piano Yamaha created especially for the show). One night of the run was broadcast around the world at movie theaters; the show was also released on DVD/Blu-ray.

63

"I FELT IT WAS SOMETHING I HAD TO WRITE"

BILLY ELLIOT: THE MUSICAL

MAY 11, 2005
(OPENING NIGHT)

Curtain call at the opening night and world premiere of *Billy Elliot: The Musical*, Victoria Palace Theatre in London.

After *The Lion King*, Elton's most successful stage musical was *Billy Elliot*, which ran for eleven years and over forty-five hundred performances in England.

The musical was based on the UK film of the same name, released in 2000. Set in 1980s England, the story concerns the determination of eleven-year-old Billy to pursue his dream as a ballet dancer despite the opposition of his father, a miner, who's dealing with fallout from the British miners' strike of 1984–1985. Elton saw the film during its premiere at the Cannes Film Festival, and was extremely moved by it, finding Billy's struggles with his father mirrored his own upbringing. "I was gobsmacked right from the get-go," he told the *Toronto Star*.

Elton's partner David Furnish had noted Elton's strong reaction to the film, and when speaking with the film's director Stephen Daldry and screenwriter Lee Hall at a party after the screening, suggested the film should be made into a musical. Elton declared he'd love to write the music, and Daldry found himself shaking hands with Elton over the idea.

Daldry wasn't the only person from the film to join the musical team. Hall agreed to write the book and lyrics, and

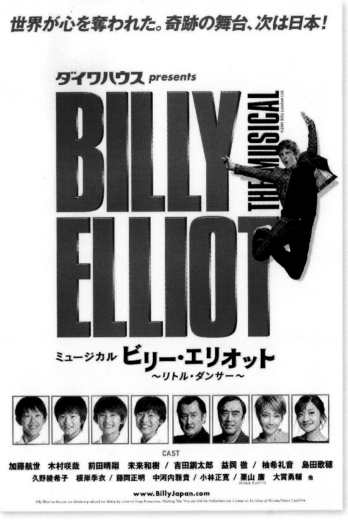

choreographer Peter Darling signed on for the stage show. Furnish became one of the producers.

Hall had never written for a musical before, but Elton had faith in his abilities and described their working relationship as "joyous and very easy." "Electricity" is an emotional highpoint, Billy describing the freedom he feels when he dances, "flying like a bird." "Expressing Yourself" is a playful number, with Billy's gay friend Michael encouraging him to push boundaries, whether that's taking ballet or wearing a dress ("What is wrong with dressing up in satin and lace?" is certainly a sentiment Elton could relate

to). "Born to Boogie" is about shaking one's booty, but it's also a nod to the music of Elton's friend, glam rocker Marc Bolan. The miners and their families are given sturdy anthems ("Stars Look Down," "Solidarity") and political commentary (the sardonic "Merry Christmas Maggie Thatcher").

Previews began on March 30, 2005, with the show's official opening date in May at Victoria Palace Theatre in London. It won four Laurence Olivier Awards (the UK equivalent of the Tony), including Best New Musical. "Electricity," from the original cast album, reached #4 in the UK charts in 2006. A 2014

performance that was broadcast live to movie theaters was later released on DVD/Blu-ray. The show opened on Broadway on November 13, 2008, to rave reviews. It would win ten Tony Awards, again including Best Musical.

"It's just as relevant now as it was when it was written," Elton declared at a tenth-anniversary celebration of the London show. "It never dates, it never gets tired, the children are amazing."

64

"AND MANY HAPPY RETURNS"

THE SIXTIETH BIRTHDAY PARTY

MARCH 25, 2007

Elton celebrated his sixtieth birthday with a concert at Madison Square Garden in New York City in March 2007. Among those helping him celebrate was Bernie Taupin (pictured).

Playing Madison Square Garden is considered a peak moment in a musician's career. When Elton first played the venerated venue on September 23, 1973, it turned out to be the first of dozens of performances he'd make there. So as his sixtieth birthday approached, there was only one place to hold the party. "I knew I had done fifty-nine shows at Madison Square Garden and I said the only place I want to be is New York City on my sixtieth birthday," he announced.

Of course, he had to work up to the celebration. Birthday festivities had kicked off earlier in the month with a party in London. And prior to the MSG show, a select group of Elton's friends had enjoyed a private birthday party at the

Cathedral of St. John the Divine. At the show itself, he was introduced by none other than former president Bill Clinton. "Thank you for coming tonight to help celebrate Elton John's joining my favorite club, the sixty-year-olds!" he joked. Clinton went on to praise not only Elton's accomplishments as a musician, but his charitable work, noting that the Elton John AIDS Foundation had worked with the Clinton Foundation to provide medicine for HIV-positive children in Kenya. "Happy birthday, friend!" Clinton concluded. "God bless you. On with the show!"

Elton, in a black tailcoat, white shirt, an enormous silver cross around his neck, and his rose-tinted glasses adding the obligatory dash of color, found the

perfect song to open with: "Sixty Years On," from *Elton John*. The first half of the three-hour, thirty-three-song set drew on deep cuts like "Ballad of a Well-known Gun" ("We haven't played this song in maybe thirty years," Elton noted). There was also a rare performance of his John Lennon tribute "Empty Garden (Hey Hey Johnny)," Elton explaining he didn't often do it live because it was "too upsetting."

Perhaps that's why the song was followed by a more upbeat moment, with comedians Whoopi Goldberg and Robin Williams (who called Elton "a man who used to make Liberace look Amish") taking the stage. They in turn introduced Bernie, who led the sold-out crowd in singing "Happy Birthday"; as confetti swirled around him, Elton joked, "Oh my God, I used to snort this stuff."

"There's nobody I have more respect and love for than him," Bernie declared, with Elton responding in kind: "Without Bernie Taupin, none of us would be here tonight, because words have always come first."

The show's second half featured big hits and crowd pleasers: "Daniel," "Bennie and the Jets," "Philadelphia Freedom." Elton dedicated "Something About the Way You Look Tonight" to his partner, David Furnish, and finished the main set with a double-barreled attack of "Crocodile Rock" and "Saturday Night's Alright for Fighting." The last song of the night, during the encore, was another appropriate choice: "Your Song," Elton and Bernie's breakthrough hit.

The entire concert was released on DVD later that year as *Elton 60: Live at Madison Square Garden*.

65

"MY BIGGEST INFLUENCE IN THE LATE 60s AND EARLY 70s"

THE UNION ALBUM WITH LEON RUSSELL

OCTOBER 19, 2010 (RELEASE)

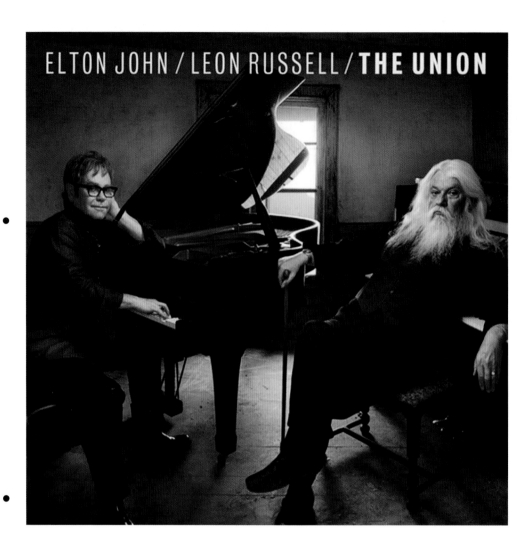

ELTON JOHN / LEON RUSSELL / **THE UNION**

Elton adored Leon Russell as a musician and admitted he was "petrified" during his August 1970 residency at the Troubadour to see Russell in the audience. He'd likely have been even more nervous if he knew that some forty years later he'd be making an album with this man he so admired.

Russell, born and raised in Oklahoma, initially worked as a session musician in LA. He went on to perform with Delaney & Bonnie, on Joe Cocker's "Mad Dogs and Englishmen" tour, and at the George Harrison–organized Concert for Bangladesh charity show. His songs "Delta Lady," "This Masquerade," and "A Song for You" were hits for others, while he had his own hits with the singles "Tight Rope" and "Lady Blue."

In the fall of 1970, Elton opened for Russell on a number of occasions, including four shows at the Fillmore East in New York (Russell played guitar on "Burn Down the Mission" during Elton's set; Elton came on to perform during Russell's encore performance of "Roll Away the Stone"). But by the twenty-first century, Russell's career was operating at a more modest level. He was also dealing with various health and financial difficulties.

While listening to Russell's album *Retrospective* during a South African holiday in 2009, Elton decided to seek out his one-time mentor, tracking him down in Nashville. The telephone conversation left Elton so inspired, he called back and asked if Russell would

like to make an album together. By November 2009, the two found themselves at The Village recording studio in LA, working with producer T Bone Burnett.

As Elton later recalled, listening to Mahalia Jackson's rendition of "Didn't It Rain" sent him to the piano to begin work on the song "A Dream Come True," Russell joined in, "And suddenly the album was definitely on and it was just gung ho from that point on." Most songs were written by Elton and Bernie, Russell also writing three and collaborating on three other numbers. There's a bittersweet quality to the album, readily seen in song titles like "When Love Is Dying" and "Hearts Have Turned to Stone." Russell adds a welcome down-home grit to Elton's polished pop sheen, and the album is also enlivened by the numerous artists who were eager to make guest appearances, including Neil Young, Brian Wilson, and Booker T. Jones.

The Union reached #3 in the US, #12 in the UK; the track "If It Wasn't for Bad" got a Grammy nomination for Best Pop Collaboration with Vocals. The album's release was followed by a short tour, and 2011 saw the release of a documentary about the making of the album, also entitled *The Union*, directed by Cameron Crowe.

The album gave Russell's career a much-needed boost, and Elton was pleased to be able to induct his friend into the Rock and Roll Hall of Fame in 2011. Following Russell's death in 2016, Elton released a statement which said in part, "He was a mentor, inspiration and so kind to me . . . I loved him and always will."

With Leon Russell on ABC's *Good Morning America* at the Beacon Theatre in New York City, October 20, 2010.

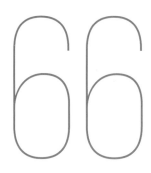

"AND OUR SPECIAL GUEST IS . . ."

"SNOWED IN AT WHEELER STREET" (BY KATE BUSH)

NOVEMBER 21, 2011 (RELEASE)

Riga, Latvia, November 3, 2011, a few weeks ahead of the Kate Bush release.

Kate Bush was thrilled. She had loved Elton's music while growing up and getting the chance to work with him was a dream come true. "I'm just completely knocked out," she told *Mojo*. "I was so excited that he agreed to do it. It was really written for him, so I didn't know what I would've done [without him]."

She was referring to Elton's vocal appearance on the track "Snowed in at Wheeler Street" from her album *50 Words for Snow*. The moody, atmospheric track is sung from the perspective of two lovers who encounter each other across the centuries, from ancient Rome to 9/11. Such an enigmatic, experimental album was perhaps an unusual place for Elton to crop up. But over the course of his career, he's made numerous guest appearances on other artists' recordings, often revealing he's not at all afraid of stepping outside his comfort zone.

It's no surprise to find him contributing an uncredited vocal on Neil Sedaka's "Bad Blood," for example. And appearing with his good friend John Lennon on "Whatever Gets You Thru the Night"? A no-brainer. But working with grunge act Alice in Chains? Probably not expected. Nonetheless, you'll find Elton playing piano on the title track of Alice in Chains' *Black Gives Way to Blue*, a moving tribute to the band's late lead singer, Layne Staley.

One especially busy day had Elton making appearances on two very different albums. The smooth-voiced Engelbert Humperdinck had written a "very sweet" letter to Elton inviting him to sing with him on a cover of Elton's "Something About the Way You Look Tonight" (for Humperdinck's 2014 album *Engelbert Calling*). Once the job was done, Elton headed three blocks down the road to where hard rock act Queens of the Stone Age were recording their 2013 album . . . *Like Clockwork* to

contribute piano and vocals to "Fairweather Friends." All in a day's work for a musician who's said he can't stand being inactive.

One of Elton's most grandiose matchups was trading vocals with opera legend Luciano Pavarotti on "Live Like Horses" for *Pavarotti & Friends for War Child* (2006), part of a series of benefit albums that raised funds for humanitarian causes. Compare that to the simpler, country-infused romp "Caroline" from Brandi Carlile's *Give Up the Ghost* (2009). Carlile was especially fond of Elton's *Tumbleweed Connection* and felt that "Caroline" had "the same funky piano vibe." She described working with Elton as an "out of body experience" to *New Musical Express*.

Other notable guest appearances by Elton include vocals and piano on "Solid Wall of Sound" on *We Got It from Here . . . Thank You 4 Your Service* (2016), the last album from hip-hop group A Tribe Called Quest; vocals for the spirited "Oh Well" from *In2ition* (2012) by 2CELLOS, a modern classical duo who also toured with Elton for a number of years; vocals on the title track of Fall Out Boy's reunion album, *Save Rock and Roll* (2013); and a breezy cover of Womack & Womack's "Teardrops" on Scottish singer Lulu's album of duets, *Together* (2002).

"I've learned something from each artist that I've worked with," Elton told the *Toronto Star*. And his desire to keep learning about new music, and work with new artists, has kept Elton an in-demand guest artist.

The enigmatic Bush, seen here in 1978, was thrilled to have Elton guest on her 1991 track, "Snowed in at Wheeler Street."

67

"LONG MAY SHE REIGN!"

THE QUEEN'S DIAMOND JUBILEE CONCERT

JUNE 4, 2012

Over the years, Elton has had a more than passing acquaintance with Queen Elizabeth II, so it wasn't surprising to find him part of the celebrations for the Queen's Diamond Jubilee in 2012, celebrating her sixtieth year on the throne.

The Diamond Jubilee Concert was just one of many related events held throughout the Commonwealth during the year, but it was certainly one of the most spectacular. A stage was built at the foot of the Queen Victoria Memorial, directly in front of Buckingham Palace. Over 1.2 million people sent in applications for one of the ten thousand free tickets made available to the public. Large screens were set up in area parks so those without tickets could also

watch live. The resultant crowds were estimated to be between a quarter of a million and half a million.

The show opened with Robbie Williams's performance of "Let Me Entertain You," backed by trumpets and drums from the second battalion of the Coldstream Guards. The acts ranged from vintage performers like Tom Jones and Shirley Bassey, to younger performers like Jessie J and will.i.am, and a few unexpected choices (Grace Jones's steamy club classic "Slave to the Rhythm").

Her Majesty wasn't seen settling into the royal box until the show's second half, when the heavy hitters came on. Welsh actor Rob Brydon introduced

Elton gamely rebounded from a respiratory ailment to deliver a three-song set at the Queen's Diamond Jubilee Concert.

Greeting Queen Elizabeth II at Buckingham Palace during the Diamond Jubilee.

Elton with a flourish: "If you're still standing, he is the Rocket Man, he is the Lion King, he is both Bennie and his Jets—Elton John!"

Elton then strode on stage, wearing a relatively restrained outfit, all in black, save for his bright pink sparkly jacket. His short set began with "I'm Still Standing," an appropriate choice at an event honoring a monarch who had ascended the throne in 1952. Elton's voice was noticeably rough, an indication of his recent health issues (he'd been briefly hospitalized the previous week because of a respiratory infection). But, ever the trouper, he rallied in the best show-must-go-on tradition.

"Your Majesty, congratulations—an incredible achievement," he said after the first number. "And we are very honored to be here tonight to play for you. Thank you." "Your Song" was next, its simple sentiment bringing a down-to-earth moment to the festive proceedings. "That's your song!" Elton shouted at the number's conclusion, in reference to the monarch.

"Now I hope you're in good voice for this one," he announced prior to his last number, building the anticipation by playing random musical passages on his piano before finally switching into the bright, upbeat tempo of "Crocodile Rock." The audience, jubilantly waving Union Jack flags, loudly sang along

during the "la-la-la" sequences, Elton at one point getting up from the piano to conduct them.

Paul McCartney's set closed the main show, and Elton returned with the other performers for his last number, "Ob-La-Di, Ob-La-Da," which culminated in another singalong. The concert came to a conclusion with "God Save the Queen" and a fireworks show.

Elton was by now such a part of the fabric of British life it was impossible to imagine such a patriotic celebration being held without him.

68

. . . .

"UNLIKE ANYTHING I HAD DONE BEFORE"

. . . .

REMIX FROM DOWN UNDER

. . . .

JULY 16, 2012 (RELEASE)

Pnau teamed with Elton again in 2021, this time on the track "Cold Heart (Pnau Remix)" with Dua Lipa.

Good Morning to the Night saw Elton really pushing the creative envelope. Or, more accurately, allowing someone else to do so.

Elton had discovered Pnau, the Australian dance music duo of Nick Littlemore and Peter Mayes (Nick's brother Sam has since joined the group) while touring Australia in 2007. In one account, he saw one of the group's releases at a Virgin Megastore at Pitt Street Mall in Sydney and purchased it because he liked the cover. In another version, he heard Pnau's "Wild Strawberries" on the radio and sent his partner David Furnish to seek out and buy the record. In any case, the next step was to track down Pnau's members. The next morning Littlemore was startled to get a phone call from Elton, asking if they could get together.

A meeting at Elton's hotel was quickly arranged. Littlemore and Mayes were understandably nervous when they arrived. "We were feeling all that weird stuff when you're about to meet a superstar," Littlemore told the *Industry Observer*. "Within 10 seconds of meeting us, he's been hugging both of us and telling us he's our biggest fan, and suddenly you feel totally relaxed. And have some tea and grapes."

Once Elton proclaimed their album *Pnau* the best record he'd heard in ten years, the group's profile received a welcome boost. The next surprise came when Elton asked them to do an album of remixes of his 70s songs with minimal input from him; he simply handed over the master tapes and told

them they could do whatever they wished. The two went on a crash course of study, spending the next six months glued to their iPods absorbing Elton's music, then discussing how they would rework it.

Pnau didn't just remix the songs, they reinvented them, creating high-energy setpieces tailor-made for the dance floor, with Elton's and Bernie's riffs and lyrics wafting in and out of the musical mix. The title track, for example, wove together elements of "Philadelphia Freedom," "Mona Lisa and Mad Hatters," "Funeral for a Friend," "Tonight," "Gulliver," "Sixty Years On," "Goodbye Yellow Brick Road," and "Someone Saved My Life Tonight" to a brisk beat. It was an imaginative way to bring new life to songs that were four decades old— modern music that still retained the original classic elements.

The album, ultimately credited to "Elton John vs. Pnau," debuted at #1 in the UK, prompting another unexpected phone call. "Elton was calling us up at 3 a.m. going, 'Why the fuck aren't you awake? We're going number one,'" said Mayes. In the US, the album reached #20 in the Top Electronic Albums chart, while the title track reached #30 in the Dance/ Electronic Singles Sales chart.

The reviews were positive. The *Guardian* called the album "Refreshingly unpredictable, this is a blueprint for what remix albums should aspire to." Elton was proud of the album even as he admitted he had little to do with it: "There was an album with my name on it at Number One and I had no idea whatsoever how it had been made."

With Pnau during their Ibiza 123 Music Festival show at Sant Antoni De Portmany, Spain, July 2, 2012.

With Pnau during their Ibiza 123 Music Festival show at Sant Antoni De Portmany, Spain, July 2, 2012.

69

LOVE AND MARRIAGE, PART TWO

ELTON WEDS DAVID FURNISH

DECEMBER 21, 2014

Elton and David, and sons Zachary and Elijah, attend a benefit for the Elton John AIDS Foundation, September 4, 2014, in Windsor, England.

Given the constant turbulence in his personal life, Elton couldn't be blamed for thinking he might never find a suitable partner. But one night in October 1993 changed everything.

Elton had been feeling at loose ends at his home in Windsor on October 30. He eventually called a friend, asking him if he could round up a few people for a dinner party. Among the small group who arrived was David Furnish, a Canadian who worked as an advertising executive for the Ogilvy & Mather agency in the London. On learning that Furnish had an interest in photography and film, Elton showed him his own photography collection, and found himself becoming increasingly interested in this new acquaintance.

At the end of the evening, he asked for Furnish's phone number. He called him the next day, and that night the two had their first date, meeting at Elton's London home for a lavish Chinese take-out dinner from Mr. Chow's. They soon became a couple. "I thought, 'God, this is new territory for me—someone wants to be with me just because he likes me,'" Elton later told *Parade*

magazine. He also liked Furnish's independence: "He had a real job, his own apartment, a car." It was, he wrote in his memoir, the first time he'd been in a normal relationship.

The *Tantrums & Tiaras* documentary showed the level of trust Elton had developed in Furnish, comfortable enough to allow himself to be filmed at his worst. And it also marked the beginning of Furnish's becoming more involved in Elton's professional life. After collaborating with Elton over the years on projects ranging from film and theater productions to the Elton John AIDS Foundation, Furnish eventually took the big step of becoming Elton's manager.

The two entered into a civil partnership on December 21, 2005—the first day civil partnerships for same-sex couples became legal in Britain. The couple became parents, with the birth via surrogate of their two sons, Zachary Jackson Furnish-John in 2010, and Elijah Joseph Daniel Furnish-John in 2013. At the time of Elijah's birth, the couple said in a statement, "Both of us have longed to have children, but the reality that we now have two sons is almost unbelievable. The birth of our second son completes our family in a most precious and perfect way." When same-sex weddings became legal nine years later, the civil partnership was converted to a marriage on the ninth anniversary of their civil partnership. The ceremony was held at their Windsor home, with Ozzy and Sharon Osbourne, David and Victoria Beckham, Lulu, and Hugh Grant among the celebrity guests. Elton posted pictures on social media throughout the day, sharing the event with a worldwide audience. "We're grateful and privileged to live in a country where it isn't illegal to be gay and where equality is a reality," he said in a statement. "Let's all stand up for LGBT people living around the world who deserve the same rights."

70

CAR TUNES

"CARPOOL KARAOKE" SINGALONG

FEBRUARY 7, 2016 (US BROADCAST)

Corden and Elton confer onstage during rehearsals for the 60th Annual Grammy Awards at Madison Square Garden, New York City, January 25, 2018.

"Carpool Karaoke" is a fan's dream come true: riding around in a car with your favorite celeb and singing along to the radio like giddy teenagers. In 2016, it was Elton's turn in the hot seat.

"Carpool Karaoke" was created by James Corden as a recurring segment for *The Late Late Show with James Corden*, a program he began hosting in 2015. He got the idea from a similar sketch he'd done for the British television special *Red Nose Day 2011*, where he sang with George Michael while riding in a car; the 2014 documentary *When Corden Met Barlow* featured another sketch along the same lines. The first "Carpool Karaoke," which aired on March 26, 2015, featured Mariah Carey.

Corden starts the segment by telephoning an off-screen friend, begging them to accompany him as he drives to work on a rainy day. The passenger side door then opens, and—surprise!—it's Elton John! So what else is going to be on the radio when it's first turned on but "Your Song." "Who'd have thought! Who'd have thought!" says Corden, before the two take up the melody.

Elton quickly gets into the spirit, enlivening "I'm Still Standing" with the appropriate hand movements. "I never knew you were such a dancer!" Corden exclaims. By "Crocodile Rock," the feather boas and sunglasses have come out, and during "Circle of Life" the two take turns wearing a lion's wig. "Tiny Dancer" and "Looking Up," the first single from Elton's recently released *Wonderful Crazy Night* album, round out the setlist.

There's also time for some entertaining chat. When asked about his worst tantrum, Elton admits it was probably when he stayed at the Inn on the Park hotel in London and called his office to complain about how noisy the wind was: "'It's too windy, can you do something about it?' It wasn't a tantrum as such, but as reality goes, it was pretty far off the chart." He also talks about his latest album ("I wanted to make a really joyful album, and I wanted to express how I was feeling with my own life"), his shopping habits ("I've never been able to buy one of anything"), and how life-changing it's been becoming a father ("Those kids have changed our life completely").

The segment's best exchange comes when Corden learns, to his surprise, that Elton doesn't own a cellphone. "So right now I could legitimately kidnap you, and you wouldn't be able to call anyone," he says. "I've been wanting you to do that for years!" is Elton's smooth riposte. He also teasingly refers to Corden as "My future husband."

The segment comes to an end with a "Don't Let the Sun Go Down on Me" that pulls out all the stops. It's a spin around town that shows a relaxed Elton at his most engaging.

71

"THEY'RE GONNA PUT ME IN THE MOVIES"

THE BIOPIC *ROCKETMAN*

MAY 16, 2019
(WORLD PREMIERE)

Rocketman is an imaginative, fanciful filmic account of Elton's life and career, recast as a lavish musical.

Elton and David Furnish had tried to get a biopic about Elton off the ground for nearly twenty years. The subject matter proved to be problematic for the studios, who wanted a story with less sex and drugs in order to secure a PG-13 rating in the US. But, as Elton told the *Guardian*, "I haven't led a PG-13 life." Indeed, his struggle with substance abuse would be a core element of the film's story.

In 2014, it looked like the project was moving ahead. Lee Hall, who'd written the book and lyrics for *Billy Elliot: The Musical*, had written a script, Tom Hardy was cast to play Elton, Michael Gracey was hired to direct, and production was set to begin in the fall of 2014. Then the US distributor pulled out of the venture. Production wouldn't begin for another four years, with Dexter Fletcher (who took over from director Bryan Singer on the successful Queen biopic *Bohemian Rhapsody*) as director. Taron Egerton was cast as Elton on the suggestion of co-producer Matthew Vaughn, who'd been impressed by Egerton's performance of "I'm Still Standing" in the animated film *Sing*. "I knew Taron was the right man when I heard him sing 'Don't Let the Sun Go Down on Me,'" Elton later said.

The film's fantasy element is evident in the opening sequences, when Elton is seen walking down a hallway wearing a typically outrageous stage outfit. But when he walks through a door at the end of the hall, he finds himself not on stage, but at a meeting for recovering addicts. The unhappy atmosphere of his childhood home is perfectly illustrated when the family—young Reg, his mother, father, and grandmother—are shown singing "I Want Love," from Elton's 2001 album *Songs from the West Coast* (Elton said that watching this sequence

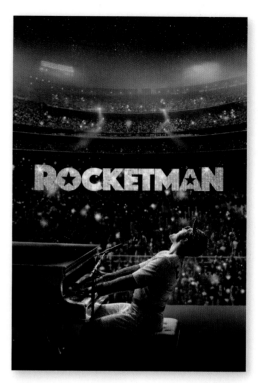

Attending the *Rocketman* UK premiere at London's Odeon Leicester Square, May 20, 2019.

for the first time moved him to tears). Linda Ronstadt had said "the place levitated" when talking about the excitement of Elton's shows at the Troubadour in 1970; in *Rocketman*, Elton, and the entire audience, do indeed levitate as he pounds out "Crocodile Rock" on the piano.

For all its campy flamboyance, *Rocketman* has a traditional story arc: shy young man finds fame, succumbs to the temptations of a rock star's lifestyle, finds redemption in the end. While the performances are strong, and it's clear the costume designer Julian Day had great fun replicating Elton's signature outfits, the film's success owes much to Egerton's star turn as Elton. His portrayal of such a complex personality is engaging and sympathetic, even when Elton is at his most petulant, not to mention that he's in nearly every scene and provides all his own vocals.

Rocketman had its world premiere at the Cannes Film Festival on May 16, 2019, and opened in the US and UK later that month to generally good notices. The film's scenes of gay sex and drug use led to its being censored in Russia and Malaysia, and it was banned entirely in Samoa and Egypt. But most reviewers welcomed the straightforward present- ation of controversial subjects, especially compared to the way Freddie Mercury's excesses had been toned down in *Bohemian Rhapsody*.

Along with such obvious contenders as "Your Song," "Tiny Dancer," and (of course) "Rocket Man," Elton and Bernie wrote a new number for the film, "(I'm Gonna) Love Me Again," which won the Oscar for Best Original Song. Overall, *Rocketman* is a playful and lighthearted overview of Elton's career, with just enough razzle-dazzle to make it shine.

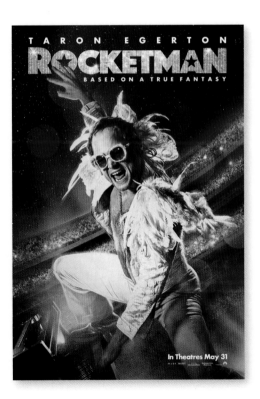

72

PAPERBACK WRITER

THE AUTOBIOGRAPHY *ME*

OCTOBER 15, 2019
(PUBLICATION)

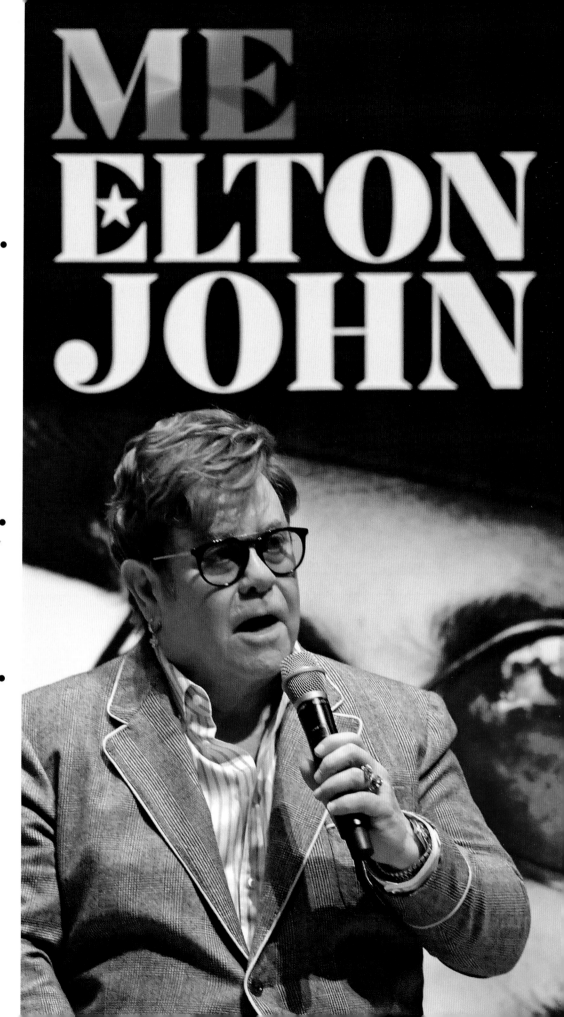

Speaking at London's Royal Academy of Music, November 19, 2019.

There have been plenty of words written about Elton. But there's nothing like getting the story from the man himself.

Me, ghostwritten with Alexis Petridis, is a lively, no-holds-barred take on Elton's life and times. It's a chatty, engrossing memoir that draws you in from the very first page and doesn't shy away from controversial aspects of Elton's life (though Petridis apparently chose to cut down on his copious swearing).

With every move he's made since becoming famous having been covered extensively, it's refreshing to read such a detailed account of Elton's pre-fame years. He paints an amusing picture of his life with Bernie Taupin when both lived with Elton's family, sharing a room where they slept in bunk beds, decorated the walls with posters, and burned incense while they listened to music: "Bernie and I could momentarily convince ourselves that we were artists living a bohemian existence at the cutting edge of the counterculture."

Along with frank discussions of Elton's relationships, health issues, and drug use (one chapter is the entire "farewell" letter he wrote to his "white lady"—cocaine), the book is packed with entertaining anecdotes. His mother watching the soft-core porn film *Deep Throat* on Elton's private plane while he toured America. Out on the town with drag star Divine and being turned away from notorious New York club Crisco Disco because they weren't dressed properly ("Whaddaya think this is? Fuckin' Halloween?"). John Lennon urging Elton not to open their hotel door when Andy Warhol knocks because he doesn't want the artist shooting Polaroids of them after they've been doing cocaine. Hosting a dinner party where Richard Gere's talking so much to Princess Diana provoked Sylvester Stallone's jealousy, nearly leading to a fight before Stallone left, grousing, "I never would

have come if I'd known Prince fuckin' Charming was gonna be here."

Elton's endearing self-deprecation ("hilariously self-lacerating," as the *Guardian* put it) brings a light touch to the tale, even when recounting more serious situations, like his suicide attempts. Though career specifics are certainly part of the story, there's little insight into his thoughts about his songwriting—the process of writing a song, working with different collaborators, and so on.

Me received good reviews and became a bestseller, moving over a quarter-million copies in the UK. But there was some legal fallout. In 2020, Elton's ex-wife Renate Blauel filed suit, claiming that parts of the memoir, and the *Rocketman* biopic (see page 182), were

"repeated and flagrant" violations of the terms of their divorce agreement. Elton's lawyers stated that the information was public knowledge and that there had been no breach of "private and confidential matters." The suit was settled in October 2020. In the words of a joint statement, "The parties are happy to announce that they have resolved this case, in a way that acknowledges Renate's need for privacy. . . . They will not be discussing each other, or their marriage, in future and will be making no further comment about the case."

Overall, it's a fun romp through Elton's life—a book truly as outrageous as its subject.

73

A BOX OF JEWELS

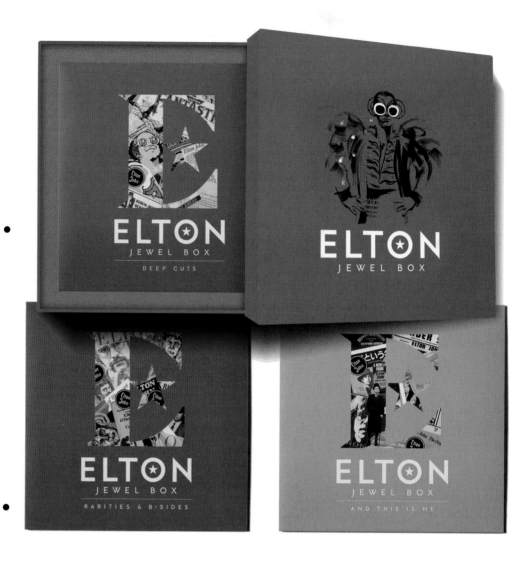

JEWEL BOX

NOVEMBER 13, 2020 (RELEASE)

What's a natural follow-up release to a box set entitled *Diamonds*? Why, *Elton: Jewel Box*, of course!

Jewel Box, released in November 2020, is Elton's most eclectic box set to date. It's not a greatest hits/best of collection. But it's not completely a rarities set either. Elton's own liner notes describe the 148-track set as presenting "an alternative history of Elton John."

The eight-CD/four-LP full set (smaller editions were also available) takes a thematic approach to Elton's career. The "Deep Cuts" discs spotlight tracks Elton feels have been overlooked. Like "Monkey Suit" from *The Union* album he recorded with Leon Russell, which he describes as something that might have

been performed on Joe Cocker's legendary "Mad Dogs and Englishmen" tour in 1970 ("lots of brass, big backing vocals"). Or "Chameleon" from *Blue Moves*, which was written for the Beach Boys (and does feature Beach Boy Brian Johnston on backing vocals). Or "All That I'm Allowed (I'm Thankful)," an homage to Philadelphia soul from *Peachtree Road*, an album he concedes "didn't really sell well but I love it, even if no one else does."

The three "Rarities 1965–1971" discs are great fun to explore. That's where you'll find "Come Back Baby," the first record Elton appeared on (as a member of Bluesology), and the first songs he wrote with Bernie Taupin, "Scarecrow" and "A Dandelion Dies in the Wind," alongside the numerous demos they recorded during those years when they were waiting for their big break. And there are some off-the-wall delights like the 1969 "Dick Barton Theme (Devil's Gallop)"/"Breakdown Blues" single by a supergroup of Elton and his session musicians jokingly dubbed the Bread and Beer Band. The discs provide the most comprehensive listening experience of Elton's pre-fame years.

The "B-Sides 1976–2005" discs serve up a reminder of the great songs to be found on the flipside of all those hit (vinyl) singles. "Don't Go Breaking My Heart" was so ubiquitous on the radio at the time of its release, few people probably realized then that if they turned the record over they'd find another duet with Elton and Kiki Dee: "Snow Queen." "Cartier," all fifty-four seconds of it, lay waiting to be discovered on the other side of the UK

"Sartorial Elegance" single (in the US, the A-side was entitled "Don't Ya Wanna Play This Game No More?"). Then there's a wild instrumental, an improvisation that came together in the studio, that was named "Choc Ice Goes Mental" and snuck out as the B-side of "Kiss the Bride" in the US.

Finally, the "And This Is *Me*" disc is best enjoyed with a copy of Elton's autobiography at hand, as each song is discussed in the book. What's interesting is that most of the songs aren't among the signature tunes that come to mind when you think of Elton John (no "Your Song" or "Rocket Man"), but rather numbers like "My Father's Gun," "Amazes Me," and "American Triangle."

The sixty-page illustrated book that's included in the set provides much fascinating information. There's a reproduction of the very Liberty

Records ad that both Elton and Bernie answered, rare photos, lyric sheets, and other memorabilia. The strong audio-visual element of *Jewel Box* makes it an excellent companion to *Me*.

Elton: Jewel Box reached #68 on the UK charts, very respectable for a box set. But it's also a release that celebrates his musical accomplishments beyond the chart statistics. It's an in-depth collection that offers an excellent summary of a remarkable career.

Performing "(I'm Gonna) Love Me Again" at the Oscars, Dolby Theatre, Los Angeles, February 9, 2020.

74

THE PANDEMIC ALBUM

THE LOCKDOWN SESSIONS

OCTOBER 22, 2021 (RELEASE)

Hosting the *iHeart Living Room Concert for America*, March 29, 2020.

Like a number of performers—Paul McCartney, Nick Cave, and Taylor Swift, to name a few—Elton used the downtime during the COVID pandemic to work on new material. What better title for his album than *The Lockdown Sessions*?

Elton was in the middle of his *Farewell Yellow Brick Road* tour when the pandemic hit, and in March 2020 he found himself with unexpected free time on his hands. He reached out to other artists about collaborating, a number of whom he'd first met when they appeared as guests on his Apple Music show *Rocket Hour*. The pandemic meant that new recording methods had to be developed as well. During in-person sessions, the performers were separated by glass panels. "Learn to Fly," recorded with the Surfaces, was the first track Elton recorded via Zoom, something he described as "totally bizarre but a great experience to try a different way of music-making!"

In fact, *new* and *different* were the watchwords for Elton's approach. "All the tracks I worked on were really interesting and diverse, stuff that was completely different to anything I'm known for, stuff that took me out of my comfort zone into completely new territory," he said in a statement at the time of the album's release. But he also noted that working with such a varying array of artists reminded him of his days as a session musician, when he had to be prepared to play a wide range of musical styles.

Some songs featured nods to his vast catalog. "Cold Heart (Pnau Remix)," which featured Dua Lipa, had lyrical and melodic references to "Rocket Man," "Where's the Shoorah?," "Kiss the Bride," and "Sacrifice" (released as the album's lead single, it topped the UK chart). Some pairings seemed obvious. Of course Elton would work well with two of the 70s' other big music acts: Stevie Wonder (the transcendent gospel of "Finish Line") and Stevie Nicks (the bittersweet, regretful "Stolen Car"). The vibrant energy of "E-Ticket," featuring Eddie Vedder, would've fit nicely on an album like *Madman Across the Water*.

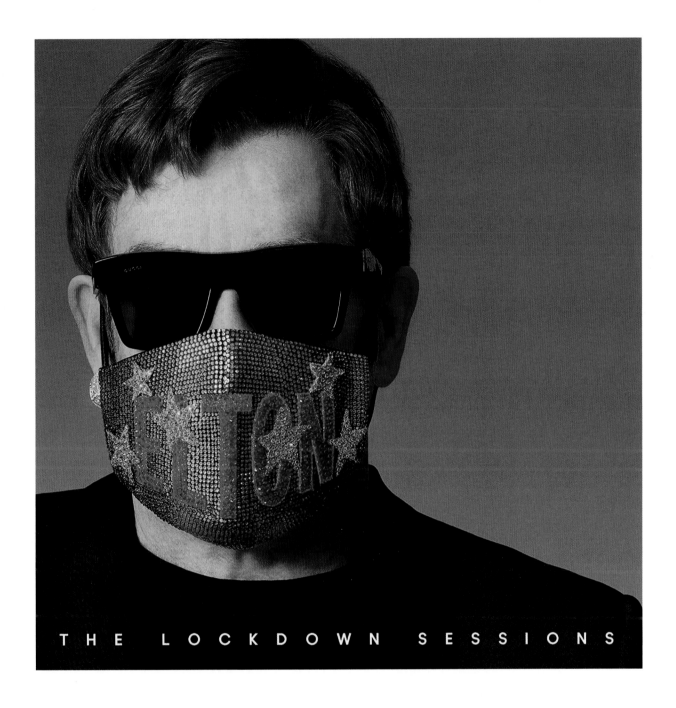

THE LOCKDOWN SESSIONS

But who would've thought to have Elton, Miley Cyrus, violinist Yo-Yo Ma, Red Hot Chili Peppers drummer Chad Smith, and Metallica bassist Robert Trujillo work together on a cover of the latter band's "Nothing Else Matters"? Or cover the Pet Shop Boys' "It's a Sin" with Olly Alexander of Years & Years? There was also a post-humous duet with Glen Campbell on "I'm Not Gonna Miss You," Campbell's poignant reflection on his struggle with Alzheimer's disease.

On its release, the album reached the Top 10 in twelve countries, including #10 in the US and topping the charts in the UK, Elton's first UK #1 since *Good Morning to the Night* (2012). "When I started collaborating with some of my favourite artists at the start of the pandemic, I couldn't have dreamt in my wildest dreams it would lead to a number one album," he wrote in a post on Instagram. "I am so proud of what we have created and thrilled that it has

connected with our fans to such a degree. It shows the spirit of collaboration and togetherness that can still happen in the most trying circumstances."

75

"THE LONG AND WINDING ROAD"

ELTON'S FINAL TOUR DATE

JULY 8, 2023

Even the Yellow Brick Road eventually comes to an end. In 2018, Elton announced he was going to make the rounds one more time in his *Farewell Yellow Brick Road* tour and then retire from touring.

The decision came about due to the changes in his family life. Now that he was in a comfortable marriage and raising two sons, he realized that if he wanted to experience the joy of watching his children grow up, he'd need to spend more time at home. Health issues (complications in the wake of prostate surgery, a serious infection picked up while on tour in South America) also made him realize that it might be time to slow the pace.

The twenty-four-song setlist for the shows, designed for maximum impact, is top-heavy with hits, and with only three post-1970s numbers (though there are a few deep cuts: "Indian Sunset" from *Madman Across the Water* and "All the Girls Love Alice" from *Goodbye Yellow Brick Road*). The band includes longtime stalwarts who've played with Elton since the 70s (Davey Johnstone, guitars, backing vocals; Ray Cooper, percussion; Nigel Olsson, drums, backing vocals), as well as newer arrivals (Matt Bissonette, bass, backing vocals; Kim Bullard, keyboards; John Mahon, percussion, backing vocals). Films by David LaChapelle and Alan Aldridge help make the show a spectacle. During "Someone Saved My

Farewell Yellow Brick Road tour, Smoothie King Center, New Orleans, Louisiana, January 19, 2022.

Life Tonight," the accompanying film shows Elton ricocheting around a pinball machine inside a ball. A film of his piano on fire provides a natural backdrop to "Burn Down the Mission." If his costumes were a bit more restrained, they were nonetheless not lacking in sparkle—his rose-covered tux accessorized with green rhinestone glasses, for example.

The tour kicked off on September 8, 2018, at the PPL Center in Allentown, Pennsylvania, and was scheduled to run for three years. There were a few hiccups along the way: two shows were canceled and a February 16, 2020, date in Auckland, New Zealand, was cut short when Elton lost his voice. Then the COVID-19 pandemic led to the tour being put on hold. The tour began again in September 2021, and at the time of this writing was scheduled to end in Stockholm, Sweden, on July 8, 2023.

Not everyone finds it easy to say goodbye. "Somebody asked me, 'What are you looking forward to, after the tour?'" Nigel Olsson told the *Los Angeles Times*. "And I said, 'The start of the next tour!' I'm hoping it's not a farewell tour."

It might be the last tour, but it's surely not the last live performance from a man who's always looking for the next adventure. His autobiography concludes with the sentence "The only question worth asking is: what's next?"

Stay tuned.

Opening night of the *Farewell Yellow Brick Road* tour, PPL Center, Allentown, Pennsylvania, September 8, 2018.

Farewell Yellow Brick Road tour, PPL Center, Allentown, Pennsylvania, September 8, 2018.

INDEX

WEBSITES

allmusic.com

eltonjohn.com

eltonjohnairdsfoundation.org

eltonography.com

en.citizendium.org/wiki/Elton_John/Discography

liveauctioneers.com/item/54593811_elton-john-rocket-man-jumpsuit

recordstoreday.com

setlist.fm

sleepingwiththepast.com

songfacts.com

walkoffame.com/elton-john/

wikipedia.org

youtube.com

IMAGE CREDITS

A = all, B = bottom, C = center, L = left, R = right, T = top

Alamy Stock Photo: 1, Nancy Kaszerman/ZUMA Wire/Alamy Live News; 7, © Christopher Harris/Globe Photos/ZUMAPRESS.com; 9, Pictorial Press Ltd.; 11TL, Keystone Press; 11BR, Antiqua Print Gallery; 13TL, Pictorial Press Ltd.; 13TR, Pictorial Press Ltd.; 15TR, Trinity Mirror/Mirrorpix; 17, Pictorial Press Ltd.; 24T, sjvinyl; 42B, CBW; 29B, amer ghazzal; 33, AF Archive; 39TR, sjvinyl; 51TL, Vinyls; 69, Historic Collection; 76, Pictorial Press; 77, Pictorial Press; 78TL, AF Archive; 79, TCD/Prod. DB; 82, Trinity Mirror/Mirrorpix; 84–85, Pictorial Press; 97, Gijsbert Hanekroot; 106, AF Archive; 107B, AF Archive; 104, Classic Picture Library; 105R, Vinyls; 112, Martyn Goddard; 114, dpa Picture Alliance; 115, David Parker; 120, Trinity Mirror/Mirrorpix; 121, Trinity Mirror/Mirrorpix; 135, Trinity Mirror/Mirrorpix; 150, AF Archive; 151, Everett Collection; 159, Fabio Diena; 162TL, Sewyn; 164, United Archives GmbH; 165TL, Vinyls; 174, Ints Kalnins/Reuters; 175T, Trinity Mirror/Mirrorpix; 208, Trinity Mirror/Mirrorpix.

AP Images: 108–109, Boris Yurchenko; 118–119, PA/PA Wire; 131, Express Newspapers; 153TR, James A. Finley; 153BR, James A. Finley; 160, Globe Photos/MediaPunch; 187, Chris Pizzello, File.

Bridgeman Images: 45T & 45B, Claude Schwartz; 99, United Archives GmbH.

Getty Images: 4–5, Michael Putland/Hulton Archive; 18T, Mondadori; 19, Michael Ochs Archives; 20,21,23, Val Wilmer/Redferns; 25, Michael Ochs Archives; 27R, Peter Sanders/Redferns; 28, Jack Robinson/Archive Photos; 34, Ron Howard/Redferns; 37B, Jack Robinson/Archive Photos; 38, Michael Ochs Archives; 39L, Michael Putland/Hulton Archive; 40T, Jeremy Fletcher/Redferns; 40B, Bentley Archive/Poppperfoto; 41, George Wilkes Archive/Hulton Archive; 42–43, Kent Gavin/Mirrorpix; 46, Ron Howard/Redferns; 50, Michael Putland/Hulton Archive; 51TR, Watal Asanuma/Shinko Music; 52B, Michael Ochs Archives; 53, Manchester Daily Express/SSPL; 54–55, Michael Putland/Hulton Archive; 56, Michael Putland/Hulton Archive; 57B, Michael Ochs Archives; 61, David Redfern/Redferns; 62, Michael Putland/Hulton Archive; 64, Tom Hill/Wirelmage; 65, David Warner Ellis/Redferns; 66–67, Ron Howard/Redferns; 68B, Michael Ochs Archives; 70T, Michael Ochs Archives; 72, D. Morrison/Hulton Archive; 75, Steve Morley/Redferns; 80, Soul Train; 86, Anwar Hussein/Hulton Archive; 93, Michael Putland/Hulton Archive; 101 Terence Spencer/Popperfoto; 111, Robin Platzer/Michael Ochs Archives; 116–117, Michael Putland/Hulton Archive; 126T, Bob King/Redferns; 127L, Fairfax Media; 129, Georges De Keerle/Hulton Archive; 132, Ebet Roberts/Redferns; 136, Dave Hogan/Hulton Archive; 139, Alain Benainous/Gamma-Rapho; 140, Michael Putland/Hulton Archive; 143, Dave Hogan/Hulton Archive; 144T, Mick Hutson/Redferns; 145T, PA Images; 145B, Ken Lennox/Mirrorpix; 146, Ebet Roberts/Redferns; 147T, L. Cohen/Wirelmage; 148, Robin Platzer/Images Press; 152, Newsday LLC; 154, Rick Diamond/Archive Photos; 156, Mike Maloney/Mirrorpix; 157, PA Images; 161, Dave Benett/Hulton Archive; 166, Michael Caulfield Archive/Wirelmage; 168, Dave M. Benett; 170, Kevin Mazur/Wirelmage; 171, Kevin Mazur/Wirelmage; 172, George Napolitano/FilmMagic; 176, Leon Neal/AFP; 177, Anwar Hussein; 179, Ollie Millington/Wirelmage; 180, Dave Benett/Elton John AIDS Foundation; 181, Kevin Winter; 183, Jeff Spicer; 184, David M. Benett; 188, FOX Image Collection; 190, Erika Goldring; 191, Kevin Mazur; 192– 193, Kevin Mazur.

Iconic Images: 31T & 31B, Ed Caraeff; 58, Ed Caraeff; 59, Ed Caraeff; 88T, Terry O'Neill; 89, Terry O'Neill.

NASA: 163TR.

© Robert Alford: 90, 91, 94–95A, 107, 122, 123–124A.

Timeline (left to right): Row 1: M*, M, Alamy, M, M, M, M, M, M, Getty.
Row 2: Alamy, Getty, M, Alamy, M, Getty, M, M, M, Getty, M, Alamy.
Row 3: M, M, Getty, M, Getty, M, M, Alamy, Alford, AP, M, Alamy.
Row 4: Getty, Getty, M, M, Getty, Getty, M, Getty, M, Getty, Getty.
Row 5: Getty, Alamy, Getty, M, Getty, AP, NASA, M, M, Getty, Getty, Getty.
Row 6: Getty, M, Getty, Getty, M, M, M, Getty.
*M = memorabilia

ABOUT THE AUTHOR

Gillian G. Gaar has written about music and entertainment for a variety of publications, including *Rolling Stone*, *Mojo*, and *Goldmine*, in addition to being a senior editor at *The Rocket* magazine. She is the author of over 15 books, including *She's A Rebel: The History of Women in Rock and Roll*, *Entertain Us: The Rise of Nirvana*, *Return of the King: Elvis Presley's Great Comeback*, and *Hendrix: The Illustrated Story*. She lives in Seattle.

BIBLIOGRAPHY

BOOKS

Buckley, David. *Elton John: The Biography*. London: André Deutsch, 2019.

Doyle, Tom. *Captain Fantastic: Elton John's Stellar Trip Through The '70s*. New York: Ballentine Books, 2017.

John, Elton. *Me*. London: Macmillan, 2019.

Norman, Philip. *Sir Elton: The Definitive Biography*. New York: Carroll & Graf Publishers, 2000

Rosenthal, Elizabeth J. *His Song: The Musical Journey of Elton John*. New York: Billboard Books, 2001.

ARTICLES

Aizlewood, John. "Me by Elton John, review: cocaine, mummy issues and dinner with Michael Jackson in the perfect pop memoir," inews.co.uk, October 14, 2019.

Amorosi, A.D. "Concert Review: Elton John Bids Fond 'Farewell' in Philadelphia," *Variety*, September 12, 2018.

"Arise, Sir Elton!," BBC News (news.bbc.co.uk/2/hi/uk_news/59754.stm), February 24, 1998.

"The Artful Dodger," *Sounds*, November 8, 1975.

Associated Press. "Samoa bans Elton John biopic Rocketman over gay scenes," *The Guardian*, June 11, 2019.

Beaumont-Thomas, Ben. "Elton John announced new album made with A-list guests in lockdown," *The Guardian*, September 1, 2021.

Brandle, Lars. "When Elton John met Pnau: The story behind an unlikely UK #1 album," *The Industry Observer*, October 11, 2017.

Brunner, Richard Kepler. "How 'Elton the Poof' shafted The Sun," mcall.com, December 18, 2005.

Carr, Roy and Charles Shaar Murray. "The Life and Times of Elton John (Part One: The Early Years)," *Rock Australia Magazine* (RAM), April 5, 1975.

"Change of Name," *The London Gazette*, January 11, 1972.

Cotter, Lucy. "Winifred Atwell: The most successful black artist you've probably never heard of," *Sky News*, October 22, 2020.

David, Caris and Lesley Messer. "Elton John's 60th Birthday Rocks New York," *People*, March 26, 2007.

"Elton John Auction Nets $8.2 Million," *The New York Times*, September 10, 1988.

Empire, Kitty. "Me by Elton John review — a landmark in the memoir genre," *The Observer*, Nov 25, 2019.

Felton, David. "Interview: Elton John," *Rolling Stone*, June 10, 1971.

Foster, Alistair. "Elton John says Billy Elliot themes still so relevant, as show marks 10 years on West End," *Evening Standard*, May 13, 2015.

Fox, Doug. "Elton John at Dodger Stadium: A Show for the Aged," theeditingroomfloor.blogspot.com, October 26, 2010.

Frankel, Glenn. "Exclusive! Brash Paper Exposed!," *The Washington Post*, October 29, 1989.

Freeman, Hadley. "Me by Elton John review — hilariously self-lacerating," *The Guardian*, October 16, 2019.

Fink, Jerry. "Kitsch is served: Elton's 'Red Piano' over the top," *Las Vegas Sun*, February 16, 2004.

Gaar, Gillian G. "Elton John and Ray Cooper formed the perfect team in Moscow," *Goldmine*, June 2, 2020.

Goldstein, Mike. "Interview with David Larkham," *Album Cover Hall of Fame* online, April 18, 2014.

Greene, Andy. "Elton John Dazzles at Farewell Tour Launch," *Rolling Stone*, September 9, 2018.

Hattenstone, Simon. "George Michael: 'I'm surprised I've survived my own dysfunction,'" *The Guardian*, December 4, 2009.

Hiatt, Brian. "Inside the 'Tiny Dancer' Bus Scene in 'Almost Famous,'" *Rolling Stone*, July 31, 2020.

Hilburn, Robert. "New rock talent," *The Los Angeles Times*, August 27, 1970.

Holden, Stephen. "*A Single Man*" review, *Rolling Stone*, January 25, 1979.

Irwin, Corey. "The Day Elton John Married David Furnish," *Ultimate Classic Rock*, December 21, 2020.

Jahr, Cliff. "Elton John: It's Lonely at the Top," *Rolling Stone*, October 7, 1976.

Jensen, Gregory. "Elton John's $6 million 'garage sale,'" United Press International, August 19, 1988.

John, Elton. "Elton John: 'they wanted to tone down the sex and drugs. But I haven't led a PG-13 life," *The Observer*, May 26, 2019.

Lifton, Dave. "How Elton John Twice Owned His Favorite Childhood Soccer Team," ultimateclassicrock.com, May 29, 2019.

Miller, Julie. "Rocketman: Elton John's Forgotten 1984 Wedding to Renate Blauel," *Vanity Fair*, June 1, 2019.

Miller, Victoria. "Billy Joel Sets The Records Straight On His Famous Falling Out With Elton John," *Inquisitr*, June 26, 2016.

Nicholas, Sadie. "Kiki Dee: I've had music in me for 50 years," *The Express*, September 17, 2013.

Ouzounian, Richard. "When Elton met Billy: How the Rocket Man wrote a hit musical," *Toronto Star*, January 28, 2011.

Penner, Degan. "Elton John's Oscar Party Turns 25," *The Hollywood Reporter*, February 23, 2017.

Rader, Dotson. "Elton John," *Parade*, February 21, 2010.

Rusk, Connie. "'I didn't want to put our relationship under pressure," *Daily Mail Online*, December 3, 2020.

Savage, Mark. "Sir Elton John and ex-wife Renate Blauel resolve legal dispute," BBC News, October 14, 2020.

Schaeffer, Christian. "Show Review + Setlist: Billy Joel and Elton John at the Scotttrade Center, Thursday, May 14," *Riverfront Times*, May 15, 2009.

Siegel, Tatiana. "'Rocketman' Takes Flight: Inside Egerton's Transformation Into Elton John (and, He Hopes, a Major Star)," *The Hollywood Reporter*, May 6, 2019.

Tannenbaum, Rob. "When Elton John became a rock star: The untold story of the Troubadour concert," *The Los Angeles Times*, May 23, 2019.

Turner, Steve. "Elton John," *Beat Instrumental*, January 1973.

Watford FC Staff. "Yellow Brick Road: The Story Of Elton John & Watford FC," watfordfc.com, November 25, 2021.

Watts, Halina. "Elton John vows to kill off his most famous song because it was 'written as a joke,' *The Mirror*, May 8, 2021.

Whipp, Glenn. "Why Elton John had Cal Worthington and his dog Spot at his Dodger Stadium show," *Los Angeles Times*, December 3, 2019.

Willsher, Kim. "For sale; 'honky chateau' where Elton and Bowie recorded classic hits," *The Guardian*, August 3, 2013.

Quarto.com

© 2024 Quarto Publishing Group USA Inc.
Text © 2024 Quarto Publishing Group USA Inc

First Published in 2024 by Motorbooks, an imprint of The Quarto Group,
100 Cummings Center, Suite 265-D, Beverly, MA 01915, USA.
T (978) 282-9590 F (978) 283-2742

Motorbooks titles are also available at discount for retail, wholesale, promotional,
and bulk purchase.For details, contact the Special Sales Manager by email at
specialsales@quarto.com or by mail at TheQuarto Group, Attn: Special Sales
Manager, 100 Cummings Center, Suite 265-D, Beverly, MA 01915, USA.

28 27 26 25 24   1 2 3 4 5

ISBN: 978-0-7603-8760-3

Digital edition published in 2024

eISBN: 978-0-7603-8761-0

Library of Congress Cataloging-in-Publication Data available

Design & Page Layout: www.traffic-design.co.uk
Cover Photo: Michael Ochs Archive/Getty Images

Printed in China